DiDA

Unit 4: ICT in Enterprise

MARTIN BARRALL & DAVE PARRY

Hodder Arnold

A MEMBER OF THE HODDER HEADLINE GROUP

Orders: please contact Bookpoint Ltd, 130 Milton Park, Abingdon, Oxon OX14 4SB. Telephone:
(44) 01235 827720. Fax: (44) 01235 400454. Lines are open from 9.00–5.00, Monday to Saturday, with a
24 hour message answering service. You can also order through our website www.hodderheadline.co.uk.

British Library Cataloguing in Publication Data
A catalogue record for this title is available from the British Library

ISBN-10: 0 340 91531 5
ISBN-13: 9780 340 91531 8

First Published 2007
Impression number   10 9 8 7 6 5 4 3 2 1
Year   2010 2009 2008 2007

Typeset by Pantek Arts Ltd., Maidstone, Kent.
Printed in Great Britain for Hodder & Stoughton Educational, a division of Hodder Headline Plc,
338 Euston Road, London NW1 3BH by CPI Bath.

Contents

Acknowledgements

Every effort has been made to trace and acknowledge ownership of copyright. The publishers will be glad to make suitable arrangements with any copyright holders whom it has not been possible to contact.

The authors and publishers would like to thank the following for the use of photographs in this volume:

p1 © Bob Krist/Corbis; **p2** © Circlestock/Corbis; **p3 (top)** UpMyStreet local area information website; **p3 (bottom)** Ferruccio/Alamy; **p10** VIEW Pictures Ltd/Alamy; **p21** Last Resort Picture Library; **p22** Rex Features; **p23** © Lynn Goldsmith/Corbis; **p27** © Ed Bock/Corbis; **p34** Motoring Picture Library/Alamy; **p56** Helene Rogers/Alamy; **p76** Graham Harrison/Alamy; **p80** © Brownie Harris/Corbis; **p90** © Shout; **p91** Dave Penman/Rex Features; **p93** Esa Hiltula/Alamy; **p94** © Wolfram Schroll/Zefa/Corbis; **p99** PurestockX, Photodisc Green/Getty Images and www.istockphoto.com; **p105 (left and right)** Photolibrary.com; **p124** Hodder Education; **p141** Janine Wiedel Photolibrary/Alamy; **p160 (left)** Screenshot © Google Inc. and is used with permission. **(right)** © BBC www.bbc.co.uk; **p161 (right)** Guardian News & Media Ltd. 2006 **(left)** © Emap; **p162** Edexcel Limited.

CHAPTER 1

Identify a business opportunity

What you will learn in this chapter

In this chapter you will learn about preparing products or services to be launched and the reasoning that businesses give to justify their creation. You will learn about methods used to ensure you reduce the risks of failure of that product or service. You will also see information on feasibility studies and **mind-mapping methods**.

The starting points

When anyone sets up a business they need to plan what they are going to do, and how much it will cost to do it. But most importantly they must have some idea that there is an opportunity for the business to succeed.

Looking at your market you need to ask these questions – Who are you going to sell your product to? And more importantly, will they want to buy it, or use your services? Is anyone else making something or providing something that's similar but at a lower price?

More businesses fail than succeed. This is often because they have failed to follow the basic business rules.

Who are you going to sell to?

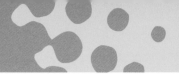

Why would anyone want to spend money on something you have produced rather than someone else's product? What is unique about your product or service?

Businesses don't always make things. They often provide a service – for example solicitors, estate agents, consultants, graphic design studios, kennels, travel agents and so on.

If your business were to produce a campaign on medical help or advice, why would people read the information? They don't have to! You need to convince them that it is worth reading. That's your job, so you need to know how to attract the audience you are targeting. If it's a charity you are promoting, why would people pay any attention to it? This, therefore, could be a good reason to do a business plan. Whether you're just starting a new business or improving an existing business, businesses should refresh their market analysis fairly often. Markets rarely stay the same: they do change, and new opportunities arise.

Business opportunities

As many people are now living longer, new business opportunities are arising from the fact that a new generation of older people has appeared.

It is a growing market that was not around 25 years ago. Markets change: your target market may be wider than just the people you already think you can reach. It's the people you strive to reach, or the people you could reach, that you need to be concerned about. Charities, which are often run as businesses, depend on people knowing about them. If they did not, no one would donate to their causes. In order to get people to give to them they need to be in the right place at the right time. They need to know their markets, but also they need to know if they can get into other markets in order to tap further funds for their causes. They would do this by researching.

New business opportunities

Getting information in order to identity the business opportunity

The information sources that will help you make a market analysis vary for every business plan. For example, you might need local information you can get from your local councils, business groups or organisations. You might also need to find some government statistics or other commercial statistics. So you may be conducting some Internet searches to track down the information.

Sometimes the information you need is going to be publicly available. You may have to make some estimates. You can produce good market research from telephone directories (such as how many other business are doing what you plan to do), catalogues, industry associations and specialist maps.

Websites such as www.upmystreet.com can produce lots of information about any area in the country – who lives there, how much houses cost, what the local incomes might be and so on.

Tracking down information

Breaking it down

When identifying a business opportunity you should always try to divide your target market into useful segments. Doing this can help a business find the more specific market needs, media, or pricing patterns in each of the different market segments.

Examples of looking for a new business opportunity

The market for a chip shop includes not just the people who regularly go there for take-away chips but everybody who lives within walking or driving distance. However, new business opportunities could include serving clubs or groups that order fish and chips in bulk for entertainment evenings.

Expanding your market

The market for a gardening business might include not only all the homes but could include commercial properties within a set area from its base. The market for downloadable music over the Internet could include everyone in the world connected to

the web, but can be targeted to specific markets by advertising. The market for personal computers includes homes, schools, businesses and government organisations. But all these businesses are looking for new opportunities to expand and increase their market share. This can be done in a number of ways but usually through careful research and design.

Car manufacturers are very good at identifying new business opportunities in a very competitive market. Often they will use the same chassis but build different bodies on top of these. For instance Volkswagen's Golf and the beetles have the same base: you can then have the Golf as a practical hatchback, an estate car, a fast GTI or a cabriolet; the beetle comes as a hard top or cabriolet. Even though both cars have the same base and same engines, they appeal to different people in different markets. Research and design have created further markets. The company has researched a business opportunity and exploited it. This type of new business opportunity thinking is called segmentation. Segmentation helps you target new people with your new business ideas. If we segment people say for delivered pizzas, then families might need a quick, reliable service, while students or clubbers might need a late-night service.

New market trends, new opportunities

You need to understand what's happening with your market (the people you intend to sell to). What trends, ideas, politics and fashions do you see having an effect on your market? If you're selling cars, for example, is there a trend that shows people are affected by higher petrol prices or other environmental concerns when they think about buying a car? There are, however, other considerations – safety, styling and layout.

With computers, is the trend towards more power and lower prices? You can easily check this out on the Internet or in magazines. How does the increase in interactive TV equipment or mobile phones affect a computer market? There was a very small market for PCs 25 years ago; now the market is what we call saturated, which means so many people have them that they are becoming harder to sell and cheaper to buy!

So how do manufacturers find new markets? Well they can introduce a variety of models – create new designs that may incorporate the computer and screen or have newer technology. They may work harder selling laptops and forget about desktop units, or simply look for new markets that need products that they can produce using their expertise. A good example was the home TV market, which was almost at saturation point (everyone has a colour TV with good sound and so on). So new products were introduced: flat-screen, wall-hung TVs were developed and priced competitively. These are now selling well – a new market was created with new products.

Mind mapping

Mind mapping is a technique which is supposed to let you make the best use of your brainpower. We also have mind-mapping software which allows you to quickly use mind-mapping techniques and harness the full range of your creative skills. The idea is that mind mapping helps you convert all random thoughts and ideas generated when you are most creative into thoughts needed most when communicating.
Mind-mapping software uses colours, images and sound to bring words and ideas to life. It is usually a graphics-based method of taking notes, brainstorming and sorting out thoughts that helps you arrange random ideas into diagrams that can be remembered. Mind-mapping software doesn't restrict your creative ideas by making you think sequentially (one thought at a time).

In general, mind-mapping software allows you to put down four important points:

✦ The idea is represented by a central image.

✦ The main themes or aims of the subject expand from a central image as main branches.

✦ Secondary themes are linked to the main themes.

✦ They are connected forming a nodal structure.

Mind maps are used all over the world. Boeing, which makes most of the world's aeroplanes, often uses a 10-metre-long mind map to help teams of aero-engineers to learn in weeks what would have taken years, saving huge amounts of money and time. Some oil companies use mind-mapping software techniques a lot in staff training programmes to improve performance at work.

It is not unusual for businesses to use mind-mapping software over a computer network. They do this to share ideas – these can then be sent via their intranet or the Internet to company branches around the world.

Feasibility study for business opportunities

This is carried out to analyse the viability of a business idea (whether it is likely to succeed or not). A feasibility study looks at answering the most important question a business will ask: 'Is it worth going ahead with the suggested project idea?' Activities of the feasibility study are directed toward helping answer this question.

Feasibility studies are used in different ways but often focus on suggested business ideas. If you have a business idea you should conduct a feasibility study to decide the likelihood of the idea working and being successful or making you money. This is always done before proceeding with the development of the business. Deciding early on that a business idea will not work saves time and money, so it's very sensible to do one! The questions that a feasibility study may answer are:

✦ Will it do all that it should for your client or company?

✦ Will the business make a good-enough profit?

✦ Will it withstand the risks it will come across?

✦ Will it stay profitable for a long time and meet targets set?

Evaluate alternatives

A feasibility study is usually carried out after discussions on a range of business ideas. The study will 'frame' and 'flesh-out' business ideas so they can be looked at in detail.

Is there a demand?

Market research may be carried out to help decide if the proposed product or service is viable in the marketplace. Market rese arch will help to find a gap or need in a market. If no need or gaps are found, there probably is no point in proceeding with a costly feasibility study. If gaps are found, a market assessment can give focus and direction to the designing of business scenarios to try out in the feasibility study.

Summing up

The results of your feasibility study should outline in detail the various business ideas examined and the strengths and weaknesses found in each. Project leaders should look at the feasibility study and challenge its underlying assumptions.

Decisions

The final decision is one of the most important – it is the point of no return. Once you have definitely decided to pursue a business idea, there may be no turning back. A feasibility study will be the most important information source in making this decision. This suggests the importance of a properly developed feasibility study.

Reasons to do a feasibility study

Carrying out a feasibility study is simply good business practice. Any successful business will not go into a new business without carefully examining all of the issues and checking the probability of business success. The feasibility study also does the following:

✦ gives sound information for decision making;

✦ focuses the idea and outlines alternatives;

✦ could find new opportunities;

✦ suggests ways you should not proceed.

Marketing plan

Before you decide to spend time and money on a business, you should know if anyone will be interested in what you make or sell. Any business will look to see if there is a market for their proposed product or idea before they set up machinery, bring in material or employ people. Marketing companies like to draw up a clear plan of the type of people they are going to sell to. They will ask them questions, look into their lifestyle, create mood boards so they know what they live like, where and what they buy, where they go on holiday and build up a practical study of the group.

Mood board

Five-year-olds are a market perhaps for toys, clothes, games, medicines and so on. Employed people are another market, which in turn can be broken down further:

- higher professional occupations
- lower professional and higher technical occupations
- unskilled.

These in turn are broken down into numbers and separated out in more detail.

Distribution of your product

You will need to know where your customers are in the world. It is very unlikely that they are all local. Most businesses use the Internet, which opens them up to a target market (the world). Products are commonly made in one country and sold in another. Many products are made near to where the raw materials are, although this is not always the case. To make your product you may need a computer and a website for a campaign to help provide information to a specific group. It could mean you need moon dust!! In which case you would have little chance of making a successful business as the raw materials are not at hand.

The word distribution includes all things to do with getting the product or service to a customer. You have to get your product either to the end customer or to the people who will be selling it for you. Distribution costs can be high so an efficient distribution system may be critical for marketing success.

Distribution methods may be:

✦ direct – direct through a sales force, Internet and so on;

✦ indirect – retailers (shops), wholesalers (people who sell to retailers) or agents;

or a mixture of all of these.

The level of market coverage may be:

✦ intensive – sells everywhere in the country, mass availability;

✦ selective – sells in most parts of the country, wide availability;

✦ exclusive – sells only in specialist outlets, restricted availability.

Places selling your services or product could be some or all of the following types:

✦ websites

✦ shops

✦ department stores

✦ markets

✦ exhibitions

✦ trade fairs

✦ wholesalers

✦ mail order.

Things that affect the distribution of your product can include:

✦ volume – quantity and timescale

✦ location of storage.

Pricing the services or products

Decisions on pricing can be complex and require knowledge of the political, competitive, market and economic conditions, and customers.

If your product is unique (has no competition), you can name your price (unlikely to happen) and if it does well it could be related to a fashion or fad item. Fashion or fad products may sell amazingly well but only for a short period of time. We have all seen children's toy fashions come and go. Shoes, clothing and accessories can all be big sellers for a while. This is OK for a business which can quickly move over to producing something else but if the business is focused on one or two products that come and go quickly they may be in trouble. The other argument about huge-selling short runs is that if you have made enough money from one you may no longer need to work again!

Factors affecting price setting

The price of the product to be sold can be fixed by you as a recommended retail price (RRP) but this can change. Cost factors can include changes in the cost of raw materials. For example plastic products are usually manufactured from an oil-based product and oil prices can fluctuate widely, so this in turn will affect the cost of such a product. Other factors may be to do with competition; competitors often reduce the cost of their products in order to attract customers.

You can justify price changes:

✦ due to excellent or bad results;

✦ due to excellent or bad research;

✦ due to strong or weak competition.

Product promotion

Promotion has to do with getting your product or service known to the people who you want to sell it to. This consists of four main areas:

✦ public relations

✦ personal selling

✦ advertising

✦ sales promotion.

You can make a timetable for promotion. Certain types of promotion (for example TV, magazine ads, trade shows) require long planning times. The promotional areas could be a mixture of special promotion programmes, such as seasonal promotion programmes – summer promotions or Christmas promotions.

Homework

1 Try to find some products that have been launched by lager companies and suggest reasons for their failure. Was it design, poor research, bad timing, political problems or competition?

2 Write up a feasibility study in 200 words suggesting that it might be a good idea to place a heliport in the local shopping centre. What good reason could you come up with? What reasons could you find that would suggest it would be a bad idea?

CHAPTER
2

Financial planning

What you will learn in this chapter

In this chapter you will learn how to model a range of financial and business scenarios using a spreadsheet.

Modern office

Introduction

All modern businesses use ICT to manage their finances. A range of professional packages is available to carry out the mathematical work, but often they are based on relatively simple spreadsheets.

Most large companies will have bespoke applications, which are designed for a specific purpose and are not usually available in shops. After working through the material in this chapter, you will have some idea of how these are put together, and the sort of calculations and functions offered by bespoke and 'off the peg' software solutions.

You will already have experience of working with spreadsheets from previous units, and perhaps from other subjects as well. In this chapter the emphasis is on developing a spreadsheet solution for a range of business needs. If you are not sure of the basics, take a look at the first book in this series.

All spreadsheets are made up of rows and columns of cells. The power of the spreadsheet application comes from manipulating the data in the cells.

In the past, businesses used a team of people to carry out the operations that a spreadsheet can do in seconds. Using a team of people can introduce all sorts of problems, including inaccuracy. Using a single spreadsheet not only provides a quicker method, but can also be more accurate in most cases.

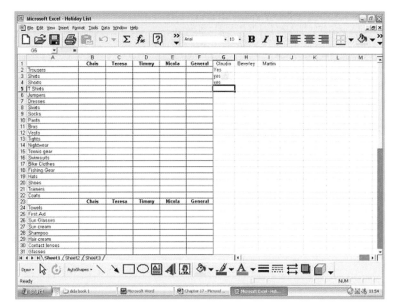

Spreadsheet application

Data manipulation

In a spreadsheet it is a straightforward operation to add a row or column of figures. This makes it easy to produce 'what if' models.

In a spreadsheet containing a list of figures in different cells, such as 1, 2, 3, 4, 5, 6, 7, 8, 9, a total could be calculated in the tenth cell using the Sum function. The figure that would be placed in the tenth cell would be 45.

The advantage of the spreadsheet is that if a calculation were used, rather than typing in the number 45, it would not matter what the figures in the other cells were. By changing one of them the calculation will automatically recalculate the total – if you were to change the third number to 27, for example, the total in the tenth cell would change to 69.

This is the basis of a 'what if' model.

In business this is a very important model, as it can form the basis of many decisions:

✦ What if the price of eggs were to rise?

✦ What if petrol prices continue to rise?

✦ What if we made 20 instead of 15?

✦ What if we paid our workers more?

The answers to these questions can be demonstrated by using a spreadsheet to model data.

For example, if a row of figures were made up from the following data, it would be relatively easy to calculate the price of the raw ingredients for a food item:

✦ flour: 32p

✦ egg: 12p

✦ margarine: 22p

✦ water: 2p

Flour	Egg	Margarine	Water	Total
32	12	22	2	(32+12+22+2) 68

In a food-manufacturing company this would be essential information, along with the cost of machinery, buildings, energy and so on.

This data can then be used to work out exactly how much it would cost to produce the food item. In this case, the raw ingredient costs are 68p. To sell the item and make a profit the company would normally add a percentage – around 30 per cent – so the spreadsheet would have another column for the cost including profit:

Flour	Egg	Margarine	Water	Total	Cost including profit
32	12	22	2	(32+12+22+2) 68	(total + 30%) 88

This simple spreadsheet can now be used to see what may happen when the variables change.

Businesses can be successful and make a lot of profit at a certain time, yet find themselves in terrible financial difficulties weeks later. Using this simple spreadsheet will illustrate the process that successful companies use to avoid such problems.

While the raw ingredients stay the same price, the company will continue to make 20p profit on each item. However, if one of the ingredients were to become more expensive, the price would need to increase to cover the costs while still maintaining the 30 per cent profit.

While this may seem straightforward, it could mean that the price to the customer becomes higher than what they are willing to pay. So the company will make

eggs	36	38	43	44	45	32
flour	12	12	12	12	12	12
margarine	22	22	23	24	23	22
water	2	2	2	2	2	2
packaging	120	120	120	110	110	120
printing	75	80	75	80	80	80
advertising	60	80	80	120	120	88
storage	65	65	65	65	70	75
transport	190	200	190	190	180	150
wages	450	450	450	400	400	400
energy	300	300	200	200	200	200
Total	1332	1369	1260	1247	1242	1181
30%	400	411	378	374	373	354
Customer price	1732	1780	1638	1621	1615	1535

alterations to the formula to ensure that the price stays within the customer's expected range and the company still makes a profit, while covering the cost of the ingredients.

This will probably mean that the profit will decrease, which would be okay for a short while, but no business can run without careful financial management, and that means making sure that profit is maximised at all times. To investigate this further, more data is needed so that patterns can be investigated.

In this spreadsheet the price of the food item increases from 1535p (£15.35) to 1732p (£17.32) – this is due to a number of the elements increasing in price over the six runs. If the company has done its market research before making the item, it will know what price the customer is willing to pay. In this case, the company knows that £17.00 is the absolute maximum it can charge. To achieve that goal there are a number of ways to manipulate the figures:

✦ The profit can be cut for the two runs where the price is over £17.00. This may cause problems with cash flow – the way in which the company pays its bills and manages its money.

✦ Wages – which represent the highest cost in most businesses – can be cut by hiring lower-paid staff, but this may have implications in terms of their skills or motivation.

✦ Elements such as advertising may be seen as luxuries – the budget for these items could be cut, but if the goods are not advertised, there may not be any customers.

✦ Transport costs, which also represent a large part of the total, can be cut back, but this may have implications for the delivery of the goods.

✦ Packaging and printing are fairly static costs, but they could be cut by using cheaper materials – this may have an effect on how the item is perceived by the customer, as well as having an impact on the shelf life of the item.

All these options can be modelled by altering the figures in the spreadsheet and seeing what happens to the customer price figure.

A more complicated way to keep the price below the £17.00 ceiling would be to increase profits in the months that the price is low and then drop the profit margin in the two months when the price is too high – over the six runs the total profit could then be maintained at 30 per cent (or more). All this can be done using a relatively simple spreadsheet to add the data together and automatically update the totals as the data changes.

The other aspect of this type of modelling is to predict how many of an item need to be sold to make a profit – this is sometimes called goal seeking. Goal seeking is when

you know there is a figure that will mean the amount sold starts to make a profit, but you are not sure what that figure is. To calculate this you need to work very carefully with the relevant data.

There is a function in Microsoft Excel® that can do this operation for you. In order to explain how it works, the following example goes through the calculation manually.

The spreadsheet below shows a company's sales figures over six months. In that time 15,700 items were sold, but some months were better than others. Note that the Share % row also has a total shown – this is not really necessary as the figures in that row are percentages and so will always add up to 100, but to check that the underlying mathematics is correct it helps to have totals wherever it is possible to show them.

	Jan	Feb	Mar	Apr	May	Jun	Total
Sales	1500	3400	1250	3200	4500	1850	15700
Share %	10	22	8	20	29	12	100

The sales manager may want to experiment with the data to see what amount of sales would be needed to make April the highest sales month. The manual method would be to increase the figure for the sales in April until the share passed 29 per cent. Bear in mind that as the April share increases the May share will decrease, so 29 per cent may be more than is actually needed.

This is fairly easy with small data sets, but Microsoft Excel® can carry this out automatically using the Goal Seek function, which adjusts the data in a range of cells until a particular solution is found. In this case, the function would carry out the same operation as a user – it would increase the sales figures in April until the Share % reached as close to 29 per cent as possible without passing it.

The concept of goal seeking is a great way of looking at spreadsheet data – as a project manager you should always be clear about what you want, but you may not always be certain about how you will get there! (For more complex goal seeking there is also a much more complex function – Solver . If you want to investigate complex patterns of spreadsheets it is worth taking a look at this function – the Microsoft® Help files will explain it.)

This operation can also be used to estimate charges, stock levels and break-even points. For example, if the company expenditure is known and there is an expected level of sales, it is possible to work out what the price will need to be to cover the costs.

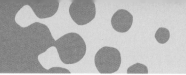

Outgoings	Sales	Price per unit
2500	20	125

This relies on careful data collection, but the manipulation of that data is still easy – it is a simple division sum: Outgoings/Sales = Price per unit. The price generated in this example is the break-even price. If each unit sold for that price, and every unit was sold, the company outgoings would be covered.

This is not a very good position to be in. If the units do not all get sold, the company will not be able to cover its costs, which means it will fall into debt. As in the examples above, there needs to be a contingency built in. Although most companies will hope to sell more than they forecast, so that they make profit they build a contingency into their price per unit, meaning that they charge a little bit extra so that they can guarantee to meet their outgoings if they generate fewer sales than they have estimated.

One of the difficulties in modelling sales and profit is the unpredictable nature of the market. In business terms, customer choice is very difficult to build in to the model. If you look at the clothing market, it is obvious that fashion trends have a massive impact on sales. Would you still wear the same style of clothes as you did two years ago? Or even worse – the same style of clothes as your teacher? Food also goes through different cycles: salads are more popular in the summer, as is ice cream, and eating habits can change following advertising campaigns. Sushi may be very fashionable at a certain time, but will it still be popular next year? Car design and colour are influenced by fashion: in the 1970s beige and green were common car colours, and black was rarely seen as it was used for official vehicles. If you take a look at a car park today you will not see many beige cars, but there will be plenty in black. The colour of kitchen appliances similarly changes over time. It used to be impossible to buy a fridge in any colour but white, for example.

Forecasting is carried out on a continual basis, as changing trends such as these make it very difficult for a company to forecast very far in advance. Stock levels are checked and materials ordered in advance to avoid manufacturing delays – any hold-up could mean that the product is delivered late, which might mean it is out of fashion before it even gets to the market!

Many companies now run a system known as just in time (JIT). This is a method of ordering materials so that they arrive on site at the time they are needed. This reduces storage costs as the materials are used and therefore converted into goods more quickly. It can also make production more efficient, but if the delivery is late, the whole production cycle can be ruined.

Project management using a spreadsheet

The previous examples demonstrate how to run simple 'what ifs', but a spreadsheet can also be used to manage a whole project, which will involve many interrelated what ifs – what if…and…or… – at the same time! Project management also has to take time into account.

Spreadsheets can be used to develop Gantt charts, which serve to check the progress of a project. The maths behind the spreadsheet can then be used to ensure that projects are delivered on budget, and if there are problems they can be spotted early enough so that action can be taken to get everything back on track.

A Gantt chart is a graphical representation of time. Each part of a project is drawn as a block taking a certain, predicted amount of time. As the project progresses, the blocks are adjusted to represent the actual time taken to carry out that stage. At the end of each block there will be a deadline – by checking progress against the blocks you can see whether deadlines will be met or missed.

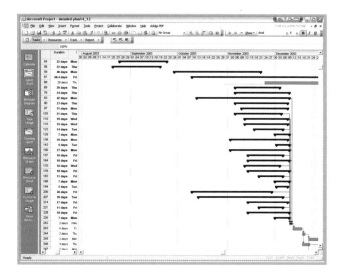

Gantt chart

There are more details on running projects in later chapters, but here we are going to look at how to set up a spreadsheet to present a Gantt chart.

Open your spreadsheet application and enter a title for the chart on the first row. Remember to make the title look like a title – increase the font size, make it bold and make sure it is clear what the chart will be about.

On the second row, in the second cell, enter a series of dates – Microsoft Excel® can generate these automatically. Enter a date in the first cell, then a second date in the adjacent cell and highlight both cells. Use the small black handle on the lower right of the highlighted cells and drag it across a number of other cells.

	01/01/2006	07/01/2006	13/01/2006	19/01/2006	25/01/2006	31/01/2006	06/02/2006	12/02/2006

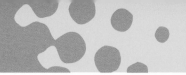

In the first cell of the third row, enter a stage in a project – usually the first stage is 'setup'.

	01/01/2006	07/01/2006	13/01/2006	19/01/2006	25/01/2006	31/01/2006	06/02/2006	12/02/2006
Setup								

If the first stage will take one week, set the background colour of the cell to something other than the default.

	01/01/2006	07/01/2006	13/01/2006	19/01/2006	25/01/2006	31/01/2006	06/02/2006	12/02/2006
Setup	▓							

Then add further stages, one for each row, and colour the appropriate cells to identify when the activity of that stage will be taking place.

	01/01/2006	07/01/2006	13/01/2006	19/01/2006	25/01/2006	31/01/2006	06/02/2006	12/02/2006
Setup	▓							
Design		▓	▓					
Construction			▓	▓				
Testing					▓			
Modification						▓	▓	
Implementation								▓

Notice in the example above that the Design and Construction stages overlap. This is often what happens in real projects: although certain stages will need to be completed before the next stage can begin, there will be times when some stages run at the same time.

This model shows the timescales necessary to complete a project. Extra data can also be included. For example, it may be useful to break down the blocks into individual days, or even hours, so that deadlines can be set more accurately. Names could be added to the stages, so that who is doing what can be tracked and checked against the deadlines. It would also be possible to add costs to each stage, so that the financial implications of running the project can be assessed at each stage.

Stage	Costs		Days	Who												
Set up working groups			1	BG												
Review of existing functions and identification of gaps; development of new procedures	£800		2	BG												
	£2100		6	HY												
	£1500		2	HY/BG												
Milestone one completed/ report				BG												
Raise invoice request/receipts			1	All												

The example above shows a more detailed chart, which contains estimated costs and the initials of staff against the activities. Behind the chart a range of formulas can be running in order to ensure that costs are correct and that the project will stay within the allocated budget. For example, everyone working on a project will have a rate of pay, which may vary for each person. To estimate the costs for the project, a formula would need to be developed to generate automatically the cost of using each person: HY = £350 per day, BG = £400 per day. So if BG worked for two days the formula would be: $400 \times 2 = 800$. By linking formulas across the spreadsheet, the costs could be tracked. The spreadsheet would need a range of data in order to do this:

✦ total estimated cost

✦ daily rates for all involved

✦ days to be allocated

✦ running totals.

If all this data were available and entered correctly, the spreadsheet would be able to automatically track the project, and by using conditional formatting it would be easy to spot when something was going wrong.

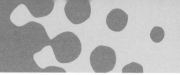

Homework

Develop a range of spreadsheets for the following scenarios:

1 Record your household shopping for a week, then use the 'what if' function to see how much your family would spend if one of the items increased in price by 20 per cent, or if the most expensive item was reduced by 30 per cent.

2 Use Goal Seek to try to get your family expenses to a particular figure – £100, for example.

3 Create a Gantt chart for planning your work on a particular project (it may be a project you are working on in another subject).

CHAPTER 3

Presenting business proposals

What you will learn in this chapter

In this chapter you will learn about presenting a business proposal. This is a way of generating support for a project. Sometimes it is straightforward, because everyone agrees that the project is important, but at other times it might be very difficult to get support, making the presentation of the proposal crucial.

Methods of presentation

As with any presentation, it is important to consider your audience and what you think will impress them, although a business proposal will always have certain elements that must be included, in an appropriate structure.

You will also need to think about how it will be presented. There are specialist applications available that generate business proposals in a format that matches the legal requirements for that sector of industry (it may be worth you taking a look at these through a Google™ search on the Internet), but this chapter looks at developing business proposals using the standard applications that most people have access to at school.

If you have the opportunity to present your proposal in person, you could use Microsoft PowerPoint® or similar presentation software, although a business proposal is often presented on paper, to be read through and discussed, rather than simply presented. This means you will need to think about putting together a professionally presented proposal, bearing in mind the following points:

◆ text – font, style, format, etc.

◆ charts – clear, accurate

◆ diagrams and images – high quality, clear and obvious.

If you get the opportunity to produce an on-screen version, you should also consider other elements:

◆ graphics – complementary, appropriate

◆ sounds – voice-over, enhancing

◆ animation – to aid explanation.

Much of the information you will need in order to prepare a professional and clear presentation, either on-screen or on paper, is explained in the other DiDA books in this series. Here are a few reminders.

Stock market

Before starting to develop your presentation, think carefully about your target audience and the media you have access to. For example, business proposals are often delivered to people concerned with financial matters – banks, finance departments, investors.

In such cases it is important that you make any financial information clear and accurate. Remember that the audience may well have more expertise than you in financial matters, so you need to make sure you have detailed answers ready for any questions they might ask.

You will need to include estimated costs, for example, and show how you have developed the estimate.

Total budget = £3500
Personnel costs = £1500
Equipment costs = £1000
Cost of materials = £1000

From these figures you might be asked the following: You have estimated the total cost to be £3500, of which £1500 is to be spent on personnel. Can you please explain how you came up with the figure of £1500? If you are presenting in person it may be relatively straightforward to explain your workings, but how would you make this information available if you were not there in person? The answers will need to be provided in your proposal.

A paper-based proposal would probably be relatively linear – you start with an introduction, move into the detail and then end with a conclusion: say what you are going to say, say it, then say what you have said. An electronic presentation gives you greater flexibility in how you allow the reader to navigate through the material.

Electronic proposal

An electronic proposal could be produced using Microsoft PowerPoint® or a similar application. As you may already be aware, Microsoft PowerPoint® is a very flexible tool, but it is often not used to its full capacity – this proposal will give you the opportunity to try out some of the more interesting aspects of presenting information.

Always start with a title slide – state your name and the title of the business proposal. Your title slide should also include the date that you are submitting the proposal and the date by which it should be agreed, so that work can begin.

Think about the audience – what sort of imagery will appeal to them? As has been pointed out throughout this series of books, the audience is crucial. Get to know what they expect and deliver appropriate material in a way that they can access easily. Try to make the presentation theme relevant to the proposal: if you are endeavouring to gain support for a charity activity, use images of the charity's work to show where the money goes; if your presentation is for a music business, select images of bands performing.

Make sure that you follow the strict guidelines on the use of images, making absolutely certain that you have any necessary permission to use them, in order to comply with copyright legislation. Seek advice if you are not sure about this.

The second slide should show something related to the end product of the proposal – maybe an artistic impression of a finished item. Take a look at the official website for the 2012 London Olympic Games

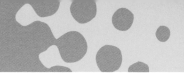

(www.london2012.org/en), which includes lots of ideas, each of which helps to justify the proposed developments.

You should also include some explanatory text. An image is a great way of showing your intentions, but without some sort of explanation it may be misinterpreted. With a business proposal, you need to make sure there are no areas where misunderstandings could occur – be accurate and precise in everything you present.

The rest of the proposal will then be similar to the paper-based proposal outlined above, that is, say what you are going to say, say it, then say what you have said.

Executive summary

The first part of a proposal, in which you outline what will be included, is usually called the executive summary – this should give clear information to the reader, quickly.

Imagine that you are presenting a proposal for starting up a new business, perhaps to the business manager of a high-street bank. He or she will listen to your proposal and perhaps ask questions or make comments, but before deciding whether or not to lend you the money, the business manager will need to discuss your proposal with other colleagues at the bank. The executive summary is what they will use to explain to others the strength of your proposal, so it must be representative of the rest of the material.

Ideally, the executive summary should be presented on one sheet of paper – or one slide. This can be difficult if the proposal is complex, so this is one rule you are allowed to break! But bear in mind that you are usually dealing with an expert audience, so if your proposal is simple, make the executive summary straightforward; if the proposal is complex, make sure the detail is reflected in the summary.

You will need to include in the executive summary a list of critical success factors (CSFs) – these are the aspects of your proposal that must be successful in order to make the rest of the proposed activity work. It is no good proposing a new train route without planning where the track will go! You should outline simple solutions here, presenting the detail later, in the main body of the proposal.

The use of colour can be helpful in highlighting CSFs – your presentation needs to be clear, so high-contrast colours are important, but if your main text is black, try experimenting with different colours for the CSFs. Make sure they stand out and that the proposed solutions are equally clear.

Read the following example. What are the CSFs? What could you suggest as proposed solutions that would make these manageable and the outcome successful?

Example

The proposal we are presenting will ensure success at Magic Animal Photography. It includes our commitment to quality and customer satisfaction. We will be responsible for ensuring a high degree of quality in three areas:

* Consistent fulfilment of the clients' expectations.

* Competitive pricing for the quality of services offered.

* A fair and reasonable profit on each portrait.

The second example is a bit more straightforward, as the proposal includes a suggestion of how to achieve the CSFs.

Example

The keys to our success are as follows:

* Service our clients' needs promptly and efficiently – all our staff have qualifications in customer service.

* Maintain excellent relationships with suppliers such as florists, hair salons and bridal shops – we have worked with the suppliers on previous projects and have an excellent track record.

* Maintain a professional image at all times – we have a dress code for staff, and all materials we use have our logo and address on them.

Main proposal

The detail of the proposal follows the executive summary, but the use of Microsoft PowerPoint®, or a similar application, means that information contained in the summary could be hyperlinked to further detail to be found later in the proposal – something that is more difficult to indicate in a paper-based proposal. For example, taking the first point in the example above:

◆ Service our clients' needs promptly and efficiently – all our staff have qualifications in customer service.

Using Microsoft PowerPoint®, the words 'customer service' could be made into a hyperlink that could jump directly to a page which details the qualifications of the staff.

A paper-based proposal would have to use page numbers to achieve the same thing:

✦ Service our clients' needs promptly and efficiently – all our staff have qualifications in customer service (page 12 has a list of staff qualifications).

If you do use a hyperlink to jump to a page in the proposal, remember to add a link back – otherwise the reader is left in the middle of the proposal and might get lost!

Reminder – adding a hyperlink

✦ Highlight the text you want to be a link, then right-click.

✦ Select Hyperlink and choose where to make the link go to – you can link to another part of the presentation or to an external document or file.

✦ When you have decided where the link needs to go, click OK and the dialogue box will disappear, leaving the highlighted text marked as a hyperlink – this is usually obvious, with blue and underlined as default settings; you can keep these settings or change them to match the other text in your presentation.

Hyperlink

The main content of your proposal must include everything that the audience will need in order to make a decision to support or refuse your proposal. If you are trying to gain support for something, there is usually a cost implication – even if it is just to convince someone to buy you a new pair of trainers!

Where money is involved you need to make sure you explain where everything will be spent, but also point out the value the investor will receive in return. If you want that new pair of trainers, how do you present a convincing argument? Do you just say, 'I want a new pair of trainers.' Or do you offer a number of reasons why getting you a new pair of trainers will actually be of benefit to the person paying for them? 'If you get me these new trainers, I will do the washing-up for a week, and I won't nag about them. Anyway, £90 is not that expensive if you think how much I will wear them – it actually works out to be less than £1 per day over three months!'

You should also try to make the content as appealing as possible, using text enhancements and other tricks that you have learnt in the previous books in this series. Where possible, include charts and graphs to present data, as these are usually much clearer than tables of figures and lend themselves to being used on-screen as well.

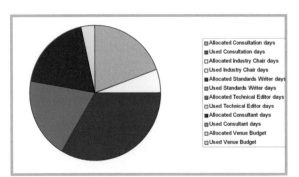

Chart

Normally you would generate your charts from your spreadsheet application – bear in mind that the chart will be made up from default colours, which may not be suitable for your colour scheme – it may be worth altering the colours in your spreadsheet application before importing the chart into your presentation. This is something to bear in mind throughout your proposal – colour can be very effective in making things clear, but it can also produce confusion. When in doubt, avoid the use of too much colour.

You also need to consider printed versions – your audience will want to take away materials so they can discuss your proposal with others. If you print out your presentation as a handout, will the colours be acceptable? Will the text still be legible?

Conclusion

The last section of your proposal should sum up what you have been talking about. As with the executive summary, this should be very positive and clear – it will be the last part that people will remember after your presentation, so it needs to leave them with a positive feeling. Highlight the benefits, so the audience leaves thinking about all the good points of your proposal, rather than any problems there may be in achieving them!

Make sure you point out how good the investment will be and emphasise why you are the right person to succeed in this activity. Try to include testimonials from other people – comments about how good you will be and how important it is that the proposal is successful.

> 'We are really pleased that the Magic Animal Photography service is coming to our area, as we enter our dogs in shows all over the country and a set of professional pictures will help to promote our dogs.' – Mrs B (Spaniels R Us)

> 'Gill has always been great at organising parties, and her staff are so professional, we will definitely be using her wedding planning service.' – Miss S and Mr G (engaged)

Preparing to present your proposal

When you have everything you need on your slides, make sure you use the spellchecker and proofread everything. A number of proposals fail because of the presentation rather than the content. Consider if you would be more likely to lend money to someone who just asked for it, or to someone who made a clear and professional presentation, explaining how the money would be used and what the benefits would be.

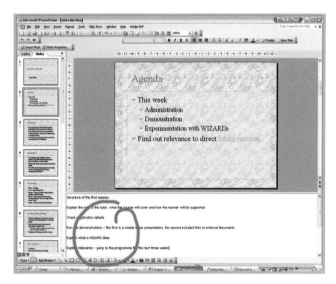

Speaker's notes

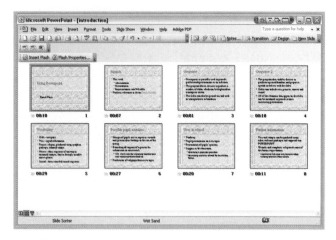

Slide Sorter

If you get the opportunity to present your proposal in person, make sure you rehearse it first, working out exactly what you want to say. Using the speaker's notes in Microsoft PowerPoint® is very useful.

If you are not able to present your proposal in person, you could record a voice-over, or use narration. Adding a voice-over is easy; it is getting the timing right that is difficult. This is usually a case of trial and error, so make sure you have some time alone to concentrate on what you have to produce.

Get a stopwatch, and some background music if you are planning to use it, along with all the appropriate equipment, such as a microphone and the presentation application, with a machine that can handle the operation. The Slideshow menu in Microsoft PowerPoint® has an option to Record Narration. This is fairly straightforward, allowing you to work through the proposal, dictating your presentation into the microphone. Your voice is recorded and when you have finished, Microsoft PowerPoint® saves the audio track and the timings you have recorded as part of the presentation. The timings are shown in the Slide Sorter view.

Before you make your presentation available to others, check it through and let your colleagues watch it. Take note of their criticisms, re-recording your narration and altering the slide timings if necessary.

Remember that you never hear your own voice the same way others do – be prepared to let someone else record your narration, but make sure you give them a very good script.

When you are happy, copy the presentation on to a portable storage media – CD or memory stick – and then you are almost ready to go.

Printed copy

Even if you are planning to present your proposal electronically, you will need to provide people with something to take away with them. There is no fixed rule here –

you have to decide how much information they will need.

It may be satisfactory to print out the executive summary or you may be better off providing handouts of each of the slides. If the proposal is for a complex business development, you may need to supply additional material that is not in the main presentation, such as details of the staff involved or addresses of suppliers. Ask other people what they think, or even ask your intended audience – before making your proposal. It may be they tell you not to bother with handouts, or they might say they want full details on the legislation involved in delivering the proposed business activity!

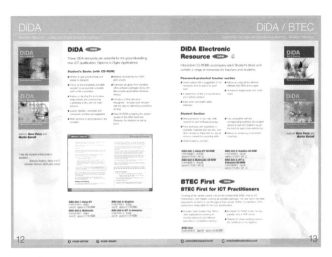

Brochure

Whatever you decide is needed, make sure you present it to the best of your ability. If you are using colour, print it in colour, and if possible use high-quality paper. Make sure that you include contact details, so that your audience can get hold of you in case they have further questions after the presentation.

Homework

1 Make a list of software applications that can be used to generate business proposals and comment on what you think is good or bad about them.

2 Use Microsoft PowerPoint®, or a similar application, to build a business proposal for something you would like to do, or choose from the list below:

✦ Build a new skate park.

✦ Take your classmates on a trip to an adventure park.

✦ Open a new healthy food outlet in your local town.

✦ Buy a set of laptop computers and mobile phones for your DiDA class.

Creating a corporate identity

What you will learn in this chapter

In this chapter you will learn about corporate identity and why it is so important to businesses to get this right. You will learn about the value of a logo and how to go about designing one, and how to design the logo part of a corporate identity and check it will work.

Corporate identity

A business's corporate identity should be linked to the bonding of ideas or principles upon which a business is built. Corporate identity is not only to do with letterheads or logos but the pulling together of a company and its products or services, and a visual and public idea of what the business is all about, which can be instantly understood.

Corporate identity is not new: knights had their signs as flags or on their armour, ships had figureheads plus the flag of the line they sailed under, pubs have always had signs showing their name and always had a picture or symbol associated with the name on a board. The idea of logos dates back to the Greeks.

'Logo' means a name, symbol or trademark designed so it is easy to recognise. Looking back at the history of logo design, it had its beginnings as a mark or a cipher made from one letter; as time went on we got a design or mark of two or more letters bound or mixed into each other. Old Greek and Roman coins have the marks or logos of rulers or towns.

The Middle Ages saw a very fast development of ciphers for church art and businesses and during the thirteenth century, trademarks for traders and merchants started to develop. Most of these marks or signs are still used today by masons, tradesmen, goldsmiths, paper makers (watermarks) and so on. The barber's symbol – hundreds of years' old – is still used today and is a red and white striped tube hanging out of their shops. Religious buildings have long had symbols and signs that immediately gave the viewer an idea of what the religion was or was about.

When people could not read, universal signs, symbols or colours made it clear to them what was going on and what was to be expected in this shop or that building.

Today's multinational companies (branches throughout the world) need to keep some kind of unity and links between the various industries they work within and the huge range of products they produce. The colours, shapes and letters they use as part of their corporate identity all help pull the range of services or goods under one big umbrella. They may use a logo, a colour scheme or a particular typeface, which they rigorously enforce on all their products throughout the world. Shell, for example, publishes details about the proportions, colours and shapes used on its logo. These must be copied exactly and the company strictly enforces the design and layout rules. This is because the company is multinational and deviations from the exact layout could weaken the company's corporate image.

The corporate identity package of a company not only brings it together, it also suggests something to the public; this may be quality, reliability, good service or safety. Therefore a glance at the logo informs the viewer what the company is, what it does and what the quality of service may be like. A driver can simply see a group of colours or a shape and instantly know the brand, quality and service they are likely to experience at a nearby service station.

Logo design

Computers have changed the face of logos and logo design. Now we have become very much aware of visual symbols, especially those used as trademarks. We are surrounded with these wherever we look – trains, buses, cars, bikes, books, magazines and posters, all have symbols on them somewhere or other.

If a company does not look professional we will probably think it is not. So it is important that a company logo looks professional, slick and memorable. Corporate identity makes us think of success and order. Business logos are always at the forefront of a business, to the public, its employees and the company itself. The logo part of a corporate identity pack is one of the strongest visual symbols a business can have and has become very important to most companies. If it is pushed forward, it can become more valuable than the company itself. Logos printed on trainers, clothing and watches mean more to some customers than the quality of the product: they have become status symbols because of what they suggest about the company and the purchaser.

Good logos are very visually readable and ensure the viewer has the brand and what it stands for in their mind straight away.

As businesses expand and sell so many different things, the need for new, one-off logos is even stronger. Graphic designers who design logos must spend a lot of their time researching and evaluating the company's present image and what image the company would like and try to bring the two together. This would normally be done via a brief. For instance, if the company wish to be seen as environmentally friendly but happen to be an oil company or power company, the designer has a real challenge. BP's newer logos are green (for obvious reasons) and try to push forward an image of efficiency and environmental awareness.

Colours and identities

Companies such as McDonald's, which started colour marketing with its yellow, and Coca Cola, which for years has used red, have found the strong links with colours make selling their products even more successful and in some ways easier for customers to pick out their products from a crowded supermarket shelf or busy street. The colours can also be used as a bond for further products from the companies and would be used on a wide variety of other items.

Recent surveys suggest that the number of brand names mentioning colours has been rising for many years. Green is the most commonly used and has strong links with environmental issues. Blue is also popular and is a strong colour to read against white (look at motorway signage). White, red and black are also very commonly used corporate colours.

Blue and green suggest calm and health. White, which represents purity and cleanliness, is widely used for electronic gadgets and goods, plus dental and health products.

Corporate identity that uses colours linked with emotion marketing can attract consumers' attention, and appeal to their emotions.

Understanding corporate identity

Designing corporate identities is a common task for a graphic designer, but sometimes the most difficult to understand.

The idea that corporate identity begins and ends with a logo, that it looks so simple and must have taken only minutes to come up with, is commonly held.

But simple or elegant design solutions are the hardest to create; it is always easier to create a complex or busy design than to create a simple shape that sums up a whole business or idea. This involves hours of research, evaluation and feedback from clients and sample groups.

A logo is only one part of a complex mix of elements that form a business's corporate identity although, in many cases, a business only requires a graphic designer to create a new logo and business stationery. But for a large company, corporate identity requires a great deal more.

The designer must think about the future flexibility of the logo. A full corporate identity brief could include the style of brochures, the shape and colours of buildings, vans, uniforms, lorries, signage, the typography and how it is used, the final finish on products (for example if they are shiny or smooth), names of the products, the linking of brands or the many aspects that affect customers' or clients' attitude to a business.

Visual identity

Creating a visual identity is important for creating an effective corporate identity. A company's image must relate to its products or services. A business that sells burgers will have a more effective image and identity using longer rounded shapes in its corporate identity than using shapes such as triangles and squares. Browns and yellows would be better to use than greens and blues; blues are rarely used on food items and food packaging.

Once a corporate identity has been established, the imagery should be consistent across all media – TV, the web, paper, card, metal and plastic. All the colours, shapes and symbols should be identifiable anywhere – on TV, in newspapers, in magazines or on the web. Fast-food businesses are great at creating effective imagery across media platforms. They always use logos, colour schemes and shapes across their TV commercials, printed media and websites. The consistency builds up a corporate identity and allows customers to quickly identify their brands.

Branding

Successful company managers set much importance on their corporate branding. Every time someone sees their logo, they form a judgement on the business and products. The effect of a slick logotype (text-style logo) is creating something in a customer's mind.

It could be, 'This company is sound, professional and I feel happy to be linked somehow to them.'

We judge the credibility of a website from things such as the quality of design, because high-quality design suggests strong investment, stability and maturity. The effect of a sloppy, poorly designed website might suggest the business is the same.

Branding is to do with creating a whole statement of the identity or ideas of a company. The company's brand should link to something bigger in customers' minds and really convince them to buy the company's product, instead of those of their competitors. A brand, therefore, is something that is instantly recognised as being part of a lifestyle, aspirations or ambition and this in turn helps sell the product by making the buyer think they are part of that.

Harley Davidson is a hugely successful brand that the company is based on. It builds large, powerful but stylish motorbikes, but when you buy the motorbike it is also suggesting you are making a statement about yourself and your ideas on life, the open road, freedom and the joining of a club. This is further backed up by the more successful marketing of a massive range of clothing and accessories, all linked and designed for the Harley Davidson brand. All Harley garages have the same colours and basic layout. All Harley dealerships have to use the corporate web design. This is all pulled together with the Harley Davidson logo, colours and logotype.

A logotype, logo script or logo is the text (typographical) and sometimes graphical mark that is the central part of the identity. It may spell out a word or become a mixture of text and shapes. Logotypes are commonly applied to goods, providing they are sufficiently strong, to motivate people to buy them simply because they are on the goods. Sports equipment, trainers, tee shirts, bags and shoes can all be sold to specific markets if they include the right logo or logo script.

Creating a corporate identity

To create a corporate identity for an organisation, you could start with a list as follows:

1   Find out about the company, business or establishment, its staff, what its aims and ambitions are. Are its services purely to make profit, is it a non-profit organisation, is it a charity, does it produce goods or services or both?

2   If at all possible, visit the business or group that you intend to design for. Talk to staff, see what they have to say and what they wish to see in the future. Look at existing design work done for them.

3   Create a design brief.

4   Use a questionnaire to create a name if the business does not already have one.

5   See if all the people involved are happy with some of your initial ideas, make sure the words you use or signs are acceptable across the world if the product will be sold or seen worldwide.

6   Show some examples of how the logotype design ideas may be used plus the thinking behind the design ideas; talk to them.

Developing your corporate identity ideas

Logos

The scalability of your logo is very important: it should be able to scale well so that it can be used on a variety of media, from business cards to billboards. Shell's logo is on oil-tanker funnels and on business cards – one is many metres high, the other is a few millimetres high.

Your logo should not be too complex or have too many fine details. This, however, is not always the case as some logos are very old and have to be used for fear of confusing customers. Heinz baked bean labels have changed but still are very similar to the older versions seen in the 1940s, 1950s and 1960s. The Chrysler logo is based on an art deco design from the 1920s and has not changed much. However, details and complexity tend to get lost when shrunk down. You will want your logo to work on tee shirts, letterheads, business cards and even merchandise such as pins, mugs or pens.

When working on the colour remember that in some printing operations, the more colours you use, the higher the cost of printing becomes. Screen-printing and litho-printing, for example, will be costed on the number of colours as part of a quote.

If you use colour, sometimes your ideas may be shown in black and white – your logo must still keep its look, feel and power. If it becomes unclear or illegible when converted to black and white, you may need to rethink your colours or tones or you could have a black and white one created that is in keeping with the colour logo.

Will your ideas be on paper, the screen or both? When you've done your final design, check it out on paper, fabric, metal, plastic and so on, besides the computer screen. Screen colours are often much brighter than any that can be reproduced on paper. Do a test print on paper and evaluate this with others. If you don't like it, look at some of the colour choices and try again using different ones.

Illustrations

Always use original artwork for corporate identify work. You could use clip art or stock images (bought-in images from image libraries) or artwork from CDs or websites providing you have permission to use them. If you create your own designs and images this is never going to be a problem.

Typefaces

Typeface can have a huge impact on the look of your logo, so choose carefully and make sure it is appropriate and readable at small sizes, and suggests the feeling of your business. Try to avoid fonts that are difficult to read such as old English or scripts. These are fine for menus or pub signs but not easy to read, especially if set in a small point size.

Usually a business has one typeface that is linked to their identity. For example newspapers and magazines will generally only use one font for all the text other than ads. They may vary the size and weight but the font is still the same. This pulls together the whole product.

Letterhead

This is the text and logo at the top of all letters usually printed on a business's letter paper. In a particular typeface, perhaps with colours, a letterhead is a very effective way of promoting a company's corporate identity. It is always worth remembering that a letterhead (despite its name) does not always need to be at the top of a letter; some of the best designs go down the side or along the bottom.

Envelopes

Matching the letterhead to an envelope is an effective way to show that your business takes its corporate identity seriously and suggests you are strong enough to take care of details.

A letterhead and business card help to build relationships with the people who help make your business a success. With a good design you can turn envelopes and letterheads into the marketing tools that keep the business running. The same goes for compliment slips that often reflect the design layout for letterheads and business cards.

Clean and simple

If you use the graphics and text on your letterhead, compliment slips and business cards to show and tell customers who you are, you need to bear in mind that because they will accompany many of your other materials, you should keep them as clean and simple as possible. (Sometimes, as we have mentioned, complex design may be appropriate.)

Business card

Try to turn your business card design into a small brochure. You could add a headline and brief text to the other business card basics – your name, title, company name, address, phone and fax number, email address and web address – and possibly a slogan. Try to limit the number of fonts; too many make your materials visually confusing. The general rule is not to use more than one serif font and one sans serif font family per document (serif fonts have 'feet', sans serif fonts do not).

T T

Try to use bold, capitalised, and italicised text as little as possible and it will have a more visually clear effect.

Design a logo for a product

Brainstorming

Produce loads of quick ideas on paper or on screen; always use colour and text together from the start if that is your aim. Bear in mind the target audience and try to get a mood board set up with images of their lifestyle applied to it. Mood boards are a basic necessity for designers to build up ideas of who they are working for. Write down ideas and if you have no specific graphic software try the drawing tools and image-editing tools (in Picture dialogue box) in Microsoft® Word. Try not to stick to your first idea but go for a range. Select one or two of the best and refine these until you have the best possible solution. When you have some ideas, ask others what they think. Check the logo is appropriate, that people feel it is right in colour or shape and that it can be scaled up or down.

Thumbnails

These are small, instant designs that result from brainstorming; you should be looking at font, colour and the important graphics.

Corrections and refining

Once you have asked others to comment on your initial logo designs, you will be required to make a decision as to which logo designs are worth investigating further. If you decide that none of your logo ideas reflect your company's identity, start developing a completely new set of logos. This is very likely to happen so do not give up but try again and incorporate some of the suggestions that may have been given to you.

The right design

After sifting through all of the changes and finally decided on the logo design which best reflects your business's vision, it is time to finalise your logo. Carry out any last touch-ups and then prepare your logo design for artwork (the finished design that will go onto everything else).

Summing up

A corporate identity should be instantly recognisable. For instance an orange shell on a petrol station says it's Shell petrol, turquoise baked bean tins with a shield on the front says Heinz, a circle with a three pointed star says Mercedes Benz. All these shapes, colours, and texts mean something to us. We do not need words – the brand is identified from the shapes and colours. The brand says it is good quality, reliable, cheap, value for money, hard wearing and so on.

Homework

1 Try to update a famous brand's logo and colours. Ask people for their comments and whether or not they think it's an improvement. Logo design is much harder that people think.

2 A new business has come up with three new additions to their range of socks. The new socks are guaranteed for two years and will not produce an odour even if worn for a week at a time – they have an antibacterial thread sewn into them! Plan a 10-point identity for the new socks called 'Notodour'.

3 Design a colour scheme and logo for a range of children's talking CDs. The colours should link to the logo, which is for the business called 'Readout'.

4 Look at some powerful logos from charities. Cut them out or copy them without any text. Answer the following questions. Have the designers got the essence of the charity into the logo design? Does the logo suggest what the charity's aims are? If it does or doesn't, explain why.

CHAPTER 5

Business communication

What you will learn in this chapter

In this chapter you will learn about the importance of communication in business and some of the methods used.

All businesses need to communicate with a variety of people, including customers, suppliers and employees. Every piece of communication has to use an appropriate method, with due understanding of the needs of the audience.

Letterheads

Companies spend thousands of pounds on designing and printing their headed paper as it is often the most common form of communication used – all printed letters will have some sort of heading, carrying the name and address of the company. It is important that this is done properly. Most large companies have very strict rules about the design and use of their letterheads and headed paper. Many will include a logo or stylised text, as well as their address and other contact details. The picture below provides an example.

This headed paper has a number of elements:

Matereality Ltd headed paper

✦ a logo – the image of an eye

✦ the company name – Matereality Ltd

✦ the registered company address – 10 House, Old Harlow, Essex

✦ phone contact numbers – 01279 4300252 and 07779 812 936

◆ email contact – dave@matereality.co.uk

◆ VAT registration number – 83992322653.

This should provide sufficient information for anybody in receipt of the communication to be able to contact the company.

TASK: Collect a number of official letterheads and take note of the common elements on all of them.

Similar information will appear on many company documents, but there may be slight differences depending on the intended use of the document. For example, a letter can be full colour and printed at a high resolution, enabling fine detail to be copied. It may not be possible to produce other documents, such as faxes, to such a high standard.

Faxes

Matereality Ltd headed paper in black and white

Fax documents are often very low resolution, about the same as on-screen images – 100dpi. Also, fax machines can only send black images on white paper.

Most companies use a fax cover sheet – a page that is sent at the beginning of a fax, so that the recipient knows straightaway who has sent it, how many pages to expect, and so on.

Microsoft® Office includes various templates for developing professional-looking documents. (It would be helpful for you to take a look at them.) One of the templates can be used as a fax cover page. It has space for a company name and logo, and fields for important information. You may be asked to design something similar for your portfolio evidence, so seeing what is already available is a good start.

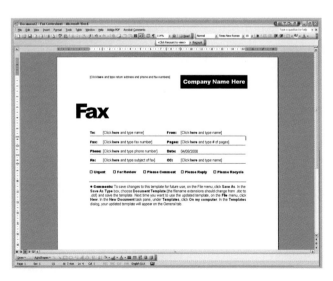

Microsoft® Word fax template

Invoices

For a company to claim payment from another person or business they need to send an invoice. An invoice is therefore a vital method of communication, as it brings in money! If it is not done properly the company may not get paid, or payment might be incorrect or delayed. This could affect cash flow, and companies with cash flow problems usually do not survive very long.

As with letterheads and faxes, there are certain common elements, such as company address, contact details and logo, but an invoice also has a range of other important pieces of information that must be included.

The invoice shown on the right includes a variety of essential elements:

Matereality Ltd invoice

- ✦ logo
- ✦ company name
- ✦ address
- ✦ VAT number
- ✦ invoice number
- ✦ customer details, name, address, etc.
- ✦ date
- ✦ order number
- ✦ code for the goods
- ✦ description
- ✦ unit price
- ✦ total price
- ✦ payment details, including bank account details
- ✦ payment deadline – 30 days from the date of the invoice.

These are arranged in a systematic way so that the customer can understand the invoice easily, and hopefully pay the bill on time. If the invoice did not contain the required information, or it was arranged poorly, the customer might not understand what to do with it and use that as an excuse not to pay the bill.

Receipt

Receipts

Another financial document that needs to be clear and accurate is a receipt. A receipt does not need quite as much detail as an invoice, but it is equally important to have accurate information set out in a clear and sensible manner.

 TASK: Look at some receipts from shops and make a note of the common elements.

Business cards

Dave Parry business card

Most companies also distribute business cards. People use them as reminders of who they have met, so it is very important that the information is clear and accurate to ensure that communication lines are opened and maintained. Imagine what would happen if two business people met and arranged to meet again, but neither of them could remember the name of the other – in normal terms this would be embarrassing, but in business it could mean that a deal was not made or a sale not closed! Business cards are a simple and effective way of getting people to remember your name.

As with all the other documents mentioned so far, the most important thing to remember when developing business cards is accuracy. For many people, the only thing they really know about a company is what they see in the business communication, and if that is messy, inaccurate or poorly put together it will give an impression that the company is poorly managed and probably not capable of providing good services or reliable products.

Designing business documents

For your DiDA qualification you may need to be able to evaluate business documentation and design material of your own. When designing documents for business there are a number of things you must consider:

1 Purpose – what is the document for?

2 Audience – who is going to read it?

3 Content and structure – what will it include and is there a pattern?

These can be broken down further, but they should form the basis of your specification.

With the three questions in mind, the designer needs to work out answers that can be used to influence their design. These answers may be straightforward or complex, but it is always crucial to find the answers.

In designing a new letterhead you will need to know what it is for. This may seem obvious, but if the letterhead also has to appear on faxes, emails or other documents you will need to think carefully about what it includes. You may also need to consider a house style.

House style

All organisations need to consider the way in which the public perceives them, and the first point of contact is often the written word – either on printed material or on a website. As this initial impression is so important, most organisations have a set of rules that cover how material is to be presented. This is known as a house style, which usually includes details about the use of logos, fonts, font sizes and styles in all public documents, along with any exceptions. Most have a similar framework:

- The 'look': all publications need to have the same look and feel – that does not mean that they are identical, but there must be common elements with which a reader will feel comfortable.

- The basic ingredients: details regarding accurate information, such as the registered address and rules about the use of a logo.

- The logo: there are very few organisations that do not have a logo.

- Colours: most organisations stipulate the colours that are used for text or logos, so that wherever their material is printed it will look the same – it is not good enough to say 'the logo is light blue and the text is dark blue'; usually specific Pantone codes would be used, such as 007CC2 for blue.

- Typeface: this details the font, font size and style that can be used – remember that certain fonts can be problematic for other users, so it is usually best to stick to standard fonts.

- White space: a logo or special text design often looks better if it is surrounded by a clear area – an exclusion zone – which is usually a proportion of the size of the logo or text.

- Placement: where the text or logo is placed is important – we read from top to bottom, so often the most important information is placed at the top of the page as it will be read first, although if it is too large it may look out of place.

In developing your own documents, or exploring those produced by others, it is important to know what the house style is and whether it has been followed. There will always be exceptions, but generally business documents should adhere to the house style.

There are also a number of other aspects to designing business documents that are considered by designers.

Presentation techniques

How a document is presented is very important. If a Member of Parliament sends a letter to an organisation or individual in a formal capacity, they will use headed paper, which will be off-white, and the envelope will match and will carry the crest of the Houses of Parliament. This confirms to the recipient that the letter is important and official – as it should be from such a place.

However, if you were sending a thank-you letter to your uncle for a birthday present he had given you, it would probably be on plain white paper, in a cheap plain envelope. This does not mean that your thank-you letter is any less important; it is just a different presentation technique designed to meet a different need – you are probably not trying to impress your uncle in the same way an MP would be in the first example.

Of course, there are a variety of different presentation techniques. If a local pizza delivery company wanted to send local residents a letter to advertise a new pizza, the first thing to consider would be cost – and that immediately means making it as cheap as possible. It would soon become obvious that sending a letter would not be the best idea. To save money on getting the message to prospective customers, the pizza company would probably use a leaflet which could be posted through letter boxes without envelopes and postage costs.

Some companies use faxes as a method of advertising. They design a fax and send it to everyone in their database with a fax number. Other companies use email, but there is so much spam on the Internet that this method is not as popular as it could be. Even so, the companies that use it have to design their material before sending it out. Of course, the Internet itself is the greatest resource for written communication, and many companies use it to great effect.

There are other methods for businesses to present information to clients or employees, such as TV and radio advertising, which also use the spoken word and imagery, even though they do not fall under the area of business documents covered here.

As a designer, you will need to hold all the information outlined above in your head – it will form your specification and help to guide your ideas. But this is only a framework; it is up to you to work out what you can or cannot do within that framework.

TASK: To help you establish what is successful and what is not, collect a range of business documents from different companies and compare them, using the following checklist (you can also add your own criteria).

- ✦ Do I know who it is from?
- ✦ Do I know who it is to?
- ✦ Describe the logo (if there is one).
- ✦ What typeface is used?
- ✦ What size and style of font have been used?
- ✦ What colours have been used?
- ✦ Does it seem fit for purpose?

Textual considerations

At the beginning of this chapter we considered a simple letterhead but if you look at it more closely you can see that a number of elements have been brought together by the designer to make the information appear in a certain way:

- ✦ The logo is set to the left, with a wide left margin.
- ✦ The company name is in a larger font size than the rest of the text, and the letter spacing has been adjusted to 'stretch' the company name.
- ✦ The email address is in blue, underlined and all lower case, following standard email styling.
- ✦ The text is all centred on the page.

You should spend some time trying to copy business documents to help you work out what the designer has done to achieve the end result – sometimes something that looks simple is actually very complicated.

Email

Using email can enhance business communication in ways that traditional printed materials cannot. As well as the design of the material, email applications can add electronic functionality, such as enabling the addition of attachments and using digital signatures.

A digital signature is an encrypted piece of data which is sent with the email and tells the recipient that it is from who it says it is, and that it has not been altered by anyone else. If a business wants to send out official documents by email, this is one way that the person receiving the document can authenticate the content. It can also be used to avoid the problems caused by spam, since the digital signature can be used by the recipient's email application to decide whether or not to accept the message – it is sometimes used to work out who is a 'friend'.

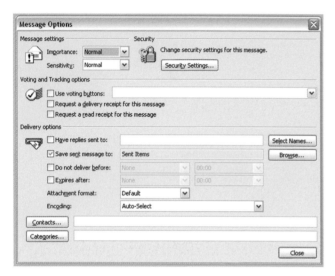

Message Options dialogue box

When sending email, the sender can ask the email application to automatically send a short message to advise when the email has arrived on the recipient's machine and when it has been read. In Microsoft Outlook® this is done using Options.

When receiving an email the recipient can set up their application to send an automated response, move the email to a specified folder or even delete it without it being read. In Microsoft Outlook® this is done using Rules.

These aspects, linked to using distribution lists (grouped email addresses), can help businesses communicate effectively and in a professional manner, as well as helping clients or employees to manage the communication efficiently.

Remember, communication must be clear and accurate for all participants – otherwise it is not really communication!

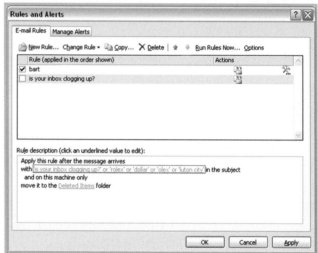

Message Rules dialogue box

Homework

1 Collect three different business documents, scan them as images and resize them to fit on a single A4 page. Make notes around the scanned image, detailing the elements that have been used to produce a professional look and feel to the documents. Try to make a set of rules that would be the house style for the documents.

2 Set up an email template that you can use for sending 'official' emails. The template must include a digital signature and a footer including a disclaimer.

Advertising and promotion

What you will learn in this chapter

In this chapter you will learn about advertising and promoting a product or service, how this is done in industry and what methods they use. There are guides and a checklist to help you get it right.

Choose the media

Anything that promotes your business could be termed 'advertising', such as a radio spot, TV advert, a brochure, a poster or a trade show. However, advertising usually means paid-for commercial messages in perhaps newspapers, magazines, radio, TV, posters, Yellow Pages or roadside hoardings.

It is very important that a business does not waste time and money advertising to people that are not potential customers. You should always make sure you choose the appropriate media for advertising so you reach your target customers.

Advertising	Promotion
This means bringing a product or services to the attention of potential and current customers. Advertising media includes TV, signs, posters, brochures, post or email messages.	Promotion involves continuous and/ or regular advertising and publicity. Often a product or service is promoted heavily to start with to get it selling, and then occasional reminders are produced to keep sales going.

Newspapers

A fairly inexpensive way to reach a large audience can be local newspapers. They are good for promoting a sale or a special deal on your product or service. The downside is that newspapers have lots of other adverts, so there's always a risk that yours may get lost in the many others that may be offering similar products.

Take a look in your local newspaper for funeral directors – how many are there? Do they all offer the same services?

Internet

Websites are great for advertising your product or service because you can use sound, images and text all together and the costs are relatively low, especially compared to TV or radio advertising. To work well your website must be kept up to date and well maintained. Websites can simply convey information about your products and service, like a catalogue, or could be fully interactive and take payments or bookings using secure systems.

Leaflets/brochures

Leaflets or brochures left in the right place (where your potential customers will pick them up) or handed out are an inexpensive way of promoting your services or products. You will have all the facilities you need to develop and produce a leaflet already – a PC, DTP software and a printer.

Magazines

Magazines offer a better opportunity to grab a reader's attention than newspapers do, but they typically cost more to show an advert. Specialist or trade magazines are helpful too because you know who will read it.

Radio

Radio is a fairly low-cost choice for advertising. It is a good way to reach a targeted market, as all radio stations are very careful in developing niche markets. Repetition is very important in radio advertising.

TV

Television advertising is very expensive as you not only have to spend a lot of money creating your advert but the cost of broadcasting it is very high. Broadcast time is sold in two ways – duration and time of day. A long advert at half-time during the World Cup Final can easily cost over £500,000.

Yellow Pages

Yellow Pages advertising is relatively inexpensive and reaches people who are ready to buy. It's a good method for local and area-based businesses, as people using the directory will usually be looking for something in their vicinity.

Outdoor

Outdoor advertising such as large posters, hoardings or smaller posters in specific places offers high visibility, and the cost is relatively low.

Before you advertise your business in any way, think carefully about what your business or service does. Think about your target market, your competition and what makes your business different. Think about the benefits of your product or service.

Advertising shouldn't just focus on features, but also on what advantages and benefits your product or service will offer the customer.

Repetition is the key rule of advertising. Research shows that the average consumer completely ignores two out of three adverts and needs nine exposures before properly remembering a product!

Layout

Graphic designers are familiar with preparing promotional and advertising material for clients. Colours, shape, text, slogans and method would all be carefully considered before design commenced. The method of delivering the messages would also be chosen as a result of careful planning and consideration as to what and where the markets might be. For instance a full-page advert in the national newspapers might not be appropriate for a local charity. Posters or using the Internet might be better.

Layout refers to the way you are going to position your design, information or text on a single medium or series of media. How you design and lay out your advertising material is of great importance. If it does not catch the eyes or ears of your market you have wasted a lot of time and money.

Borders can sometimes confuse and cram in too many ideas. However, use one when you want to frame and draw attention to something like a table of contents, a calendar or a special note. You can draw attention to boxes or images by using a drop shadow on a frame or border. Use your judgement to decide whether it is cluttering

up your design or not. Lines or rules can help divide up or separate part of your design and can help emphasise what you want to push forward to the viewer.

Designing for newspapers and magazines

The upper right-hand corner of any European newspaper or magazine is the most expensive place to put an advertisement because that's where our eye goes to first when we open a paper or magazine. The least valuable space is at the bottom left-hand corner, especially on a double-page spread, because it is the last place our eyes stray to when reading printed material. Therefore important messages should go to the top right. The web is slightly different but this rule of thumb is still generally correct. On the web we are able to place animations and movies to attract the eye to places you can not on printed material.

Points to consider

Try to use strong images or text (unless a softer approach is required) and make sure your message stands out. Space around the message is as good as anything for focusing the readers' attention.

Contrast always works: 'reversing out' (white on a black background amidst a sea of white) often catches the readers' attention. Reversing text is a good and quick way of adding impact to your ads. Never use small or thin type styles as these may disappear on the screen or during the printing processes.

Remember the very best ideas need refining, so always be prepared to make changes for the better and never hold onto something because it took ages to do if it's not good enough!

Always try to be consistent and create a house style if possible. Many leading companies use one font only and a few colours to keep the reader in contact with the company and to make recognition easy.

Always, always ask a friend or teacher for help in reviewing your work. Never present a final idea without having a review.

The very best designs and the very best solutions are often the simplest!

Columns, grids and rules

Columns and grids work well for magazines and newspapers and help web designers create a consistent look to their pages. Bear this in mind when designing for both.

Try to keep columns fairly narrow; wide columns can be tricky for the eye to follow, which is why newspapers use narrow columns for people to read on the move.

There is not always a good reason to use rules (lines between text) but sometimes they can help, for instance when you want to separate two parts of a feature. However, lines do not help emphasise parts of a text nor do they help draw the eye; if anything they make it more difficult to read. As we have already said, space often is better for pulling the viewer in, be it round text or an image.

Headlines

If you are creating a website or a static Microsoft PowerPoint® presentation some of these rules may be useful to help guide your work in the right direction. Ads need to grab the reader's attention; this can be done with headlines.

Some newspapers have headline writing down to a fine art. The Sun, for instance, plays around with words to create humorous but captivating headlines. Try to write short, clever headlines of six to eight words for ideal results.

Subheadings are useful to break the body of text (main text) into smaller, easier-to-read sections.

Space

The basic rule for space is use it! Leave lots of space around type and graphic elements. This helps draw the eye into the information. If you are designing for print, bear in mind most printed matter has larger margins at the base than at the top. You can make space between your image or text to create negative space or shapes consisting of space.

Typography (letters and text)

Use the following rules for improving legibility and readability:

✦ A common mistake is for inexperienced designers to use too many different typefaces – use one or two at the most. You can always use bold, italic and colour to break it up if you need to.

✦ Most readers find upper-case text more difficult to read than lower-case text, so never use capitals for body text (the main reading parts).

✦ Decorative text is always trickier to read than plain text.

Hyphenation, orphans and text wrapping

A copywriter will create a slogan or sum up in words what their client wants the message in the advertisement to convey to the reader. A typographer or graphic designer will then design the layout and styles for the text. Two things they would always avoid are hyphens, which can mess up the flow of text (so turn them off in

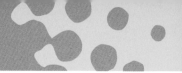

your software options' boxes), and orphans, which is a word or short line at the top of a column or on the next page all on its own.

Beware of text wrapping fever! Text wrapping has to be used carefully; you can find this option in Microsoft® Word on the Picture toolbar. Often it makes reading much more difficult. Text wrapping needs extra work to make it look good.

Kerning and spacing

Better-quality magazine and newspaper adverts always have kerned lettering: the designer has adjusted the space between letters to make them look visually balanced.

If you look for visual gaps between letters or numbers, you will see that they may be different according to the shape of the adjacent letters (for example TA, VA, eT, aW).

Example of kerning

Checking the words

Try to use someone who did not write the text to proofread your text – to check for spelling and grammatical mistakes. You can always use your spellchecker to check your text for misspelled words but these often put in the wrong word, so you still have to re-read your work. It's very easy to overlook your own mistakes, but easy for others to spot them!

Colour

The basic colours we see are red, yellow and blue. Mixed together they create all the other colours we see. Graphics programs use red, green and blue which, when mixed by being close together on the screen, give us the colour we expect to see.

Use your colour and type carefully. Try to contrast the two. Look for clues around you. Motorway signs have a blue background with white writing – easy to see in all weather conditions. Red signifies danger or excitement, greens and blues have a calming effect. Bright red walls and a purple carpet in a dentist's waiting room would probably scare most people off – yet it is still only colour.

The packaging of many food products is designed to exclude blue, a colour which is fairly unusual in food.

Younger children like bright, vibrant colour schemes whereas older people like warmer and softer tones. Beige is a favourite for over-60s' shoes and clothing.

Colour can look different on the screen and often disappoints when it comes out of a simple printer onto poor-quality paper. Coated papers, which resist being soaked by the inks, give strong colours. If you are using the web or a slide show, colours usually tend to look strong and crisp as they are illuminated by the projector or monitor.

If your text does not contrast with its background it probably will not be very readable. Therefore always try to contrast the two. Also make sure the text is big enough so it doesn't get lost in the colours around it. Small text with serifs will lose clarity.

Black and white

Often overlooked by classical styles, black and white graphics, which include grey, can look stunning. Newspapers until fairly recently were all in black and white and many still are. Black text on a white background is very clear and easy to read. Most books and magazines still use black and white for text.

Promotional checklist

✦ Make sure your message is simple and clear.

✦ Is it easily understood? Too much information will not be effective.

✦ Make sure there is a large headline. Good headlines are very important to the success of advertisements. In the print form of advertising 80 per cent of the readers go no further than the headline.

✦ Make sure that your advertisement describes your product or service precisely.

✦ Always include your contact details or where to get the service or product.

Research

Keep a file with promotional material or adverts that your competitors have produced. The material may seem irrelevant to you but may give you clues about colours, text positioning and layout. See what your competition is doing by getting people to take notice of their work.

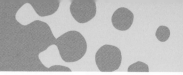

Homework

1   Gather up some flyers that are popped through your letterbox. Try to analyse them to see if they work. Make a simple checklist:

   ◆ easy to find product (contact details)

   ◆ clear message (what is on offer)

   ◆ readability (easy to read)

   ◆ and anything else you can think of.

2   Cut out a newspaper ad – the bigger the better. Lay a piece of tracing paper over the top and fix with masking tape. Look at the details – placing of text, images, space and focal point. Then cut it out and see if you can make it any better by recomposing it.

3   Find some newspaper or magazine ads. Look for power words, slogans and headlines. Do they work? If so, why? What has the designer done to make the words shout out?

CHAPTER 7

Promotional websites

What you will learn in this chapter

In this chapter you will learn about what makes a good promotional website and why it is so important to follow the rules.

A promotional website is used to promote or advertise something, rather than simply supply information. For example, the website for PC World (www.pcworld.co.uk) is a promotional website, whereas the BBC News website (news.bbc.co.uk) is an information site. However, just to add a layer of confusion, most promotional websites do provide information as well, and most information-based websites also carry advertising!

As part of your DiDA work you will probably need to produce a promotional website for something, so over the next few pages we are going to look at what needs to be done and how to go about getting it right.

Accessibility

This aspect of web design is mentioned in the other books in this series and should be a major part of your design work. You must ensure that any website or web page you produce is accessible to everyone, and meets the requirements of any regulations in this regard.

Just to recap:

✦ Use high-contrast background and text colours.

✦ Ensure all images have appropriate ALT tags.

♦ Try to avoid using frames.

♦ Where animation is used, add a description of what is happening.

A related aspect is when the site is accessible. In the past the Internet was not very reliable in terms of websites being online all the time. Nowadays this is less of a problem as most Internet servers are running at 99 per cent uptime or more. This means there is no real reason for your promotional site not to be online 24 hours a day, every day of the year.

Maintenance

You will need to consider maintenance, however. A bricks-and-mortar shop is closed at least some of the time, allowing employees to clean the shelves, reorganise and restock.

An online shop does not have time to do these things, so it is important to keep things simple and make sure you have access to an offline version that can be worked on and swapped in if something needs to change. A web design application such as Macromedia Dreamweaver® has an offline cache and an online copy. This means that the designer can work on the offline version, making any changes and updates, or just general 'cleaning and dusting'. When they are happy with the amendments, they can save and upload it, and it immediately overwrites the online version so that users see the new version when they refresh their browser. All web design applications have a 'preview in browser' option, which allows the designer to see what effect the changes will have before uploading the page and overwriting the original.

Larger, 'managed' sites, such as www.gcseinengineering. com, www.gcseinmanufacturing.com or www. gcseinappliedscience.com, have a specialist web design application called a content management system (CMS). The CMS contains a template for each page, which cannot be altered by the web team. The web team can only alter the content. When the content needs to be changed, there is a sequence of events that must be worked through before the updated page goes live.

1 The web team is notified that a page needs updating and new content is supplied.

2 The template for the page is opened from the offline archive of published pages.

3 The template is checked to make sure it is the correct page and then a copy is saved in a drafts folder.

4 The archive version is closed and the draft version is opened.

5 The draft version is made editable – as its default setting is locked.

6 The changes are made to the draft version.

7 The draft version is previewed in the browser and checked by the person doing the updating. If everything is okay the draft version is published.

8 The draft version is deleted and the published version is sent as a copy to the online server and to the archive.

9 Before a user can see the updated page the published version must be approved – this means it is checked by the manager of the web team and then put online.

10 The live server refreshes the page by overwriting the existing page and making the new page available online.

Having a system like this in place means that lots of checks are made before anything goes public. This is important for companies as they need to ensure that their online presence is always accurate and appropriate. This system also means that different people are responsible for different aspects of updating the pages:

✦ The content providers produce text and images to add to the page. They work to strict guidelines on font size, text colour, language to be used, resolution of images and image size.

✦ When the content has been submitted, the web team works on the page but does not alter content unless an obvious error is spotted, which would then be checked with the content provider.

✦ The updated page is finally checked by the web manager, who has overall responsibility to ensure that the update meets the requirements of the content provider and the general web guidelines. If everything is approved, the page can be released to the public.

A system like this is really important, but it can slow down updates. It may take more than 24 hours to update a page. The advantages of such a system are that the site can be worked on by a number of people at the same time, and as each page has to be checked before being released, it means that the final page is usually accurate.

The sites that you will be developing will probably be unmanaged, meaning that you work on the pages and upload them, and as soon as they are on the online server they will be live to the public.

Structure

When you are designing a promotional site you need to think about a number of things, many of which are common across all types of website:

✦ What software will be used to work on the site?

✦ Where is the content coming from?

✦ How many pages will there be?

✦ How will a user navigate the site?

There are also aspects that will be specific to your site, such as the visual design – what sort of look and feel will the pages have?

A promotional site should be interesting and stimulating – to grab a potential customer's attention and hold it. As the designer, it is your job to use the facilities available to you to the best effect, to produce a website that attracts lots of people and, hopefully, lots of sales. To do this you need to understand your limitations. Make sure you know how to put the software available to you to the best use – Macromedia Dreamweaver® is used by the majority of professional designers, so it should be sufficient for your needs. It may be worth spending some time looking at the templates and guides available through the Macromedia Dreamweaver® support sites, most of which offer free examples. Macromedia (Adobe) also offers free downloads of templates and additional components. Even if you adjust them to your own design, using a template will make it easier to develop a unified look and feel across your site.

Take a look at the Learn2 site (www.learn2.co.uk), which was built using a standard Macromedia Dreamweaver® template.

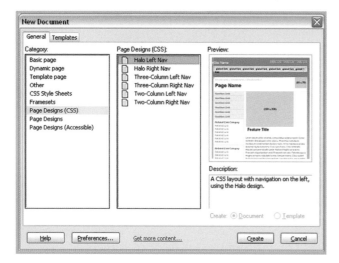

Macromedia Dreamweaver templates

Another site to look at is www.nweacc.ac.uk, which uses a simple template with a heading image and a series of drop-down menus, with the main content displayed in the lower three-quarters of the screen. This site is also very easy to navigate as the heading is the same on every page.

The designer who developed the NWEACC site obviously felt that maintaining a common style across the site was important – a good idea when developing a site that has a lot of pages. You can also see from both these sites that the corporate image, including a logo, is important.

Both sites have navigation systems, but they work in very different ways. The Learn2 site is relatively complex, using a list of links down the left-hand side of the main content area, as well as a sequence of buttons across the top. There is also a breadcrumb system that a user can utilise to trace their way back to where they came from. The NWEACC site appears much simpler: every page has the same header, with the same drop-down menus, and each menu has a list of links to other pages within the site. This means that a user can get to any page from any page and jump about in any order.

You need to consider which form would be best for your site. The best way to do this is to work on paper. In the centre write the name of the home page, and around it place the names of every page that you might want to link to directly from the home (or index) page. Beneath each of these secondary pages you can list further pages that would be linked to from them, but which would not have direct links from the home page. You could continue with this, level by level, until you have included every page. The diagram to the right provides an example of this method for a shoe-shop website.

NWEACC web page

Internal links diagram for shoe-shop website

When you have decided on the links and structure of your site, you will need to think about how a user will navigate the different pages. You can use a variety of methods, but whichever you decide on, remember to keep it simple! Make links stand out, use buttons that are obvious and, if you are using a navigation bar, make sure it is visible at all times.

Spend some time looking at different sites on the Internet and see how they organise their navigation – do they use navigation bars or buttons? You may come across sites that use hot spots on images – these can be great fun for gaming sites but will probably be too confusing for a promotional website.

Communicating with the user

An important aspect of promotional sites is how they link to the user. How can the user communicate with you, the site manager? You may have a variety of monitoring software running in the background of your site to record hits, page loads, duration of stay and so on, but have you given the user the option to get in touch with you or place an order?

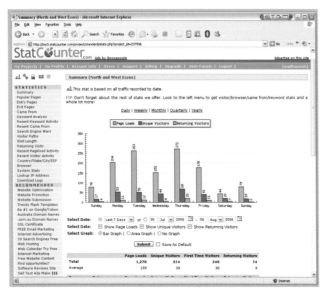

StatCounter web page

To record data about who is using your site is relatively simple nowadays. In the past you had to be a genius programmer to write special scripts to work in the background, but now there is a range of companies that will monitor your site for you and produce detailed statistics. Try www.statcounter.com if you want to see the types of service available.

In a similar way, using forms or making secure payments has developed from a very complicated system to something that is built in to a number of common software packages. Microsoft FrontPage® and Adobe Acrobat® both have a forms section, for example. You could always design your own forms in Macromedia Dreamweaver® – although getting the responses delivered to you might be difficult.

By far the easiest way of receiving information from the user is via email. Nearly every website will have an email contact point – and yours should have one too. If you set up every page to have an 'email me' link, which opens a simple email, you will soon start getting messages. As with the navigation bars discussed previously, you should make the email link very obvious.

> If you have seen anything you like on this page, please email me

Email link

One thing to bear in mind is that email is not secure, so never ask for payment or any financial details using email. If your site is going to be selling products or services online, you will need to set up a secure server link to handle credit card details and any other personal data. This can be an expensive route. To cut costs you could look for a provider offering secure server technology in the hosting package, or you could research on the Internet for companies providing secure payment systems.

Page design

Once you have considered all the technology that could be used on your site, it is time to start designing the individual pages. The best way to do this is to plan the pages using storyboards, which describe what each web page will contain.

Page reference	Content	Images, interactivity, links
Index	Welcome to the high-heel shoe site. We hope you find what you are looking for. We have over 100 items for sale on the site. Please take a look around and email me if you see anything you like.	Image of shop front Links to other pages Email link

Once you are satisfied with the storyboards, you can start to build the pages. You should remember some of the rules of earlier work: try to develop a house style for your pages, make sure that your content is accurate and clear and, above all, be honest – users will soon work out if you are exaggerating or trying to fool them!

When all your content is in place, and you have checked it by previewing the pages, you will need to get it online – it is only then that you can fully check the pages and see how the site appears on other machines.

Tip

For details on how to develop websites using Macromedia Dreamweaver® and other applications, you may want to look through the other books in this series as well as Chapter 18 of this book.

Testing

If you really want to get some good feedback on your site, let people use it! The more people you can get to use your site and give you feedback, the easier it will be to work out what is successful and what is not, and what you can change to make it better. You will have tested your site and previewed everything before launching it, but you may have been blind to some of the errors – let others look at what you have done and tell you what they think.

If you have forms working on the site, use one as an evaluation form. Otherwise, use email or even sit with people using the site and ask them questions about it, such as:

✦ Do you know the name of the company? Is it clear?

✦ Do the links work?

- Can you find things easily?

- Is the information accurate?

- Does the site feel up to date?

- Do you know how to make contact with the company?

Use the responses from these questions to check your work and direct further developments.

Finally, remember to keep your site up to date, and 'dust' it regularly – like a real shop. Customers like to see smart new pages!

Homework

1   Take screenshots of ten sites you have found. Annotate the screenshots to highlight the navigation method. Describe the layout and anything you can identify as common across the pages.

2   Develop a promotional site of your own: put together the storyboards, build the pages and then get people to use the questions listed above to evaluate your site – you may like to add some questions of your own to the list.

Presenting a business proposal in an e-portfolio

What you will learn in this chapter

This chapter deals with very important issues and will help you avoid disasters. You will learn how to create your e-portfolio so it is accessible and easy to navigate around. You will learn what methods you can use to back up your work so you always have spare copies of files in case something goes wrong.

Introduction

The key word here is organisation – the way you organise your work and the way you will present it to any viewer. You will present evidence of your achievements by exhibiting them in an e-portfolio. The portfolio is similar to an artist's portfolio except yours will be filled with electronic files and saved on a computer. The way you organise this is important. It is also important that you back your work up so there is absolutely no chance of it getting lost, overwritten or corrupted. Remember that you may be working on this for some time so you will need to organise yourself and your work over many weeks to ensure your work is safe – no work means no marks. It is your responsibility as part of this course to make sure disasters do not happen and you can only do this if you know how to copy folders and subfolders to disk or to send them via email for safe storage. Have a look at emailing work to yourself – sounds a bit odd? Well Google's Gmail™ is free and allows you to save an enormous amount of work – gigabytes of it!

Your work will be assessed by your teacher against a set of criteria from the subject specification (and then sent electronically to the exam board).

For your work to be assessed, you must submit an e-portfolio on or before the deadline date. Unlike most other subjects, for DiDA you must submit it electronically –

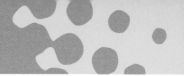

an e-portfolio. You save all your work onto a computer and never need to print anything out.

The e-portfolio must contain everything that you want to have assessed. If it is not in it, it won't get marked, and you won't get the credit for it – you may even fail the course because of it.

Before you start to compile your e-portfolio, you must ensure that you know exactly what you need to include. Your teacher will advise you on this. But you should also make sure you have looked through the guidance from Edexcel. For up-to-date information look on:

www.edexcel.org.uk
http://dida.edexcel.org.uk/home/

Making folders and organising files

On computers, there are two main types of items that need to be organised. The first, a folder or directory, is an object that can hold files or other folders. On the screen, a folder looks like a yellow or blue paper file folder.

Files and folders

The second object is a file. This is anything you save, which may be a picture, a document, a video clip or any piece of data. A file is really your work and is saved into a folder. Folders can hold thousands of files. I could have used a folder called DIDA Pics to put all the pictures in for this book, or I could have used a folder called Book 2 that has all my documents for Book 2 in it.

Naming files and folders

Windows file and folder names can contain over 200 characters, including spaces. You will probably not need to use all of these. The best thing to do is to name your files (your work) so you can find them easily. For instance a picture of your pet could be called 'Tom the cat in the garden'; another one might be 'Tom the cat on the windowsill'. Make sure the name of the file represents what is in the file. Try to keep your file names to 20–30 characters if you can. File names are followed by a full stop '.' and three letters, called an extension. Usually, the program that you are using will automatically add the extension when you save the file. You may see the extension depending on the way your computer is set up.

Filing system

If your filing cabinet is full with files and they are not in any order, you will have to spend a lot of time finding things. If your computer files or folders become full and disorderly, it will not only cause you to not be able to find things, but it also can sometimes cause problems with your PC.

The very first thing you must do is to set up an organisation system by making folders to hold your files. You will probably want to make folders for the different types of work that you do, such as school or college, home, DiDA and so on. Or you might want to separate your folders by the type: sound, videos, pictures, diagrams, web page images and so on.

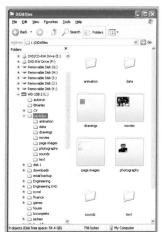

Files in order?

Folder tree

The usual file diagrams use a tree-like structure, which is sometimes called a nested arrangement. The tree has one big trunk with lots of branches. The branches then have many smaller branches, and the smaller branches have leaves. Think of your hard disk like the trunk of a tree. Most computers only have one hard disk, but as some trees have two or three trunks, so may a computer have two or more hard disks or one hard disk that is broken up in several parts known as partitions.

We will only consider the main hard disk, although you may be saving work to a networked computer. Your hard disk is called C: or the C: drive.

To view the hard disk layout, go to Start, click on My Computer then click on the C: drive. Once opened the hard disk folder will show that it has other folders inside it. To make a new folder, click on File in the menu at the top of the screen, select New and Folder. A new folder will show with 'New Folder' highlighted. Type in the name that you want to give the folder. The words that you type will appear under the

folder. If the folder still reads 'New Folder', right-click on the folder, select Rename, and retype the name again.

Folders can contain lots of other folders. If you have created a new folder called DIDA, you may want to create several folders in that folder called webs, presentations and so on. To create a folder within a folder, simply open (double-click) a folder before you choose the File , New Folder option or right-click in the folder contents, click New, then select the Folder option.

You can drag folders into each other using your mouse the same way as you can drag files into them.

Default folders

Each time you write a letter or make a new spreadsheet or a presentation, you are making a file. If you save that file, unless you say otherwise, the application you are using places the file into a particular folder, known as the default folder. Microsoft Windows® programs like Word, Works, and Excel® use My Documents as the default folder. It is a good idea to keep your files in the My Documents folder and create subfolders (folders within folders) in My Documents to suit.

Navigation

When you are ready to start to build the e-portfolio you need to arrange it in such a way that your teacher and the moderator can find everything easily. This means that you will need to develop some sort of folder and file structure, with a *contents* document with links showing where each piece of DIDA information can be found.

Usually you will have a range of documents or different files that are grouped together as a website. Each file is then linked to a 'homepage' and can be found from there.

Homepage

The main user interface of your e-portfolio will be the homepage – so make sure it works. Try to make your homepage as interesting and professional looking as you can. Use all the techniques you have picked up through the course to impress your teacher and the moderator. Make sure it's easy and clear to work through.

The homepage should be of a standard file type, such as html, and will contain a number of important details, as well as carrying a short description of the files or documents.

8 Presenting a business proposal in an e-portfolio

HOMEPAGE DETAILS:

Name

Candidate Number

Centre Number

Project title

Date of submission

Group name/Teacher name

Short description of what materials are available in the e-portfolio

Short description of each material, with a hyperlink to the file or document

A well-designed homepage is a great advantage in your e-portfolio; you could build a smart page, with rollover buttons and interactive messages, or keep it plain and simple. Whatever you decide, you should introduce the reader to what they are about to see. Try welcoming the reader.

Welcome to my e-portfolio. Over the past three months I have been working on a project – 'Producing material for a new pre-school play-centre project'. The page links below will take you to a variety of documents detailing the process I worked through and the outcomes I generated in trying to satisfy the various requirements of the project brief.

Each folder contains an index with a set of links to each file within the folder. Each link has been tested before submission. If there are any problems, you can email me at martin@e-portfolio.co.uk.

<button>Images – Here you find ten images of materials I produced for this project:

1. a design for a logo (to appear on the headed notepaper)

2. four versions of the headed paper and logo designs

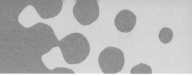

3. a postcard to be sent to prospective customers

4. a poster to appear in a local public centre

5. a handout to be distributed in a shopping centre

6. an on-screen presentation

<button>Project Planning – Here you will find the documents I used to plan and control the project:

1. Initial Plan

2. Time Sheet

3. Revised Plan

4. Quality Review Record

5. Diary

<button>Information Sources – This folder contains three files: a list of my bookmarks with short descriptions of each site, a detailed bibliography including all the magazines and books I have used and a list of images and image galleries I have visited in developing my work:

1. Bookmarks

2. Bibliography

3. Image Library

<button>Data Manipulation – In developing my ideas, I carried out a variety of research, including a survey and two interviews. The results of this research is contained in these files:

1. Questionnaire

2. Results

3. Interview Script

4. Interview One Transcript

5. Interview Two Transcript

<button>Communicating Information – The main aim of this project was to produce material that communicated information about the new play centre to the public. These files show how I have done this:

1. Document templates

2. Website designs

3. On-screen presentation of the scheme and opening times

4. Pricing documentation

<button>Review – This section holds some of the most important documentation, developed from my research, testing and evaluation:

1. Original Specification

2. Quality Review Record

3. Testimonials from the staff

4. Overall Evaluation Document

5. Proposals for future work

This homepage must be stored in your root directory and clearly identified. Give it a name that will mean something to those that view it – ordinarily a homepage would be called index.htm, but on this occasion the page can be called something else, as it will not actually be a web-based page.

You should use something like your initials, candidate number and unit number – for example DP_01234_Unit01.htm.

Within the root directory you should set up a folder structure that enables easy navigation.

Possible structures

The specification contains details on the marks available for each piece of work. However, to help your teacher and anyone else who needs to assess your work, Edexcel have broken the marks down into six categories.

Category	Available marks
Plan and manage the project	0–5
Select and capture information from a variety of sources	0–7
Collate and analyse data to produce information	0–7
Present and communicate information	0–9
Present evidence in an e-portfolio	0–9
Review the project	0–5

You may be able to use variations on these six categories as your folder titles. Or you may wish to break your e-portfolio into other sections, related to the evidence type each folder contains, such as:

✦ Images

✦ Spreadsheets

✦ Databases

✦ Paper publications

✦ On-screen publications

Each folder should contain an index page, with links to each file, making navigation very clear.

Each file must be clearly titled and saved in a format that can be easily accessed through a fifth-generation browser.

Bear in mind that the marks mentioned above for the e-portfolio are awarded across all of the material you submit.

Audience

You should keep your *intended audience* in mind at all times – your teacher, assessor and moderator. These people may not know you or your work, so the only chance you have of letting them see your best and most applicable material is by very clear navigation around your e-portfolio.

A list of acceptable file formats will be issued by Edexcel, with the project brief. These are likely to be pdf for paper-based publications, jpg or png for images, html for on-screen publications and swf (Adobe Flash® movie) for presentations, but these may be revised to take account of future developments.

To enable you to be able to work with these file types, you will need access to conversion applications. Your teacher will provide guidance on what is available to you in school. For home use, you should have access to:

✦ a compression application, such as WinZip® or StuffIt®;

✦ a pdf generator, such as NovaPDF;

✦ a Microsoft PowerPoint® to Adobe Flash® converter, such as FlashPoint;

✦ image conversion, available through most image manipulation software, such as Adobe Photoshop®.

The total file size of the e-portfolio may be around 15 MB. You must work out exactly what you need to include and then keep a close check on the size of the folder containing the e-portfolio. You may be able to keep file sizes smaller through using optimisation or compression formats.

You must present your e-portfolio content in a format appropriate for viewing at a resolution of 1024 × 768 pixels.

As with all websites, you must ensure that your materials follow the rules on accessibility.

Where possible you should:

✦ provide alternatives to auditory or visual content;

✦ avoid using colour for navigation;

✦ use simple, appropriate language;

✦ use tables;

✦ design your materials to work on any platform;

✦ provide clear navigation systems.

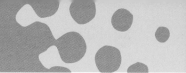

Before you submit your e-portfolio, test it! Carry out tests on a number of different machines running different browsers. Just because it works once, this does not mean it is reliable, and your qualification is resting on the reliability of your e-portfolio.

Clear identification

Each file must have a distinct title and a short explanation of its content. Remember – you will know what everything is, but will someone who looks at your work for the first time?

There may be similar problems with other file types. If you experience difficulties, it might be worth generating a short page of text as the main link, and then using a hyperlink from that to the file.

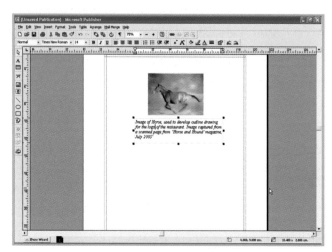

Image of horse, used to develop outline drawing for the logo of the centre. Image captured from a scanned page from 'Horse' magazine, July 2006.

The data contained in the database has been collected from the questionnaire I distributed to prospective customers. It contains the responses from 50 people.

The fields are:

- First name
- Second name
- Address 1
- Address 2
- Address 3
- Postcode
- Question 1
- Question 2
- Question 3
- Question 4

Question 5
Question 6

The query has been set up to collect the names and addresses of everyone in Luttersfield, so that I could use that information for a mailmerge to address the postcards that were sent to these people.

To view the data table, <u>click here</u>
To view the query results, <u>click here</u>
To view the merged addresses, <u>click here</u>

None of the address details relate to real addresses to avoid potential Data Protection issues.

You will see from the example that it is important to make the reader aware of any legal issues that you have had to take into account during your work. Any data that contains names and addresses comes under the Data Protection Act, so unless you have permission, you must not pass these details to others.

There may also be copyright or other issues that you have had to deal with. If you have scanned an image, have you asked permission? If you have used some text from a book, have you recorded where it came from and acknowledged it in your work? Do you have permission to use photographs of people in your images folder?

Answers to these questions should be included in the commentary that accompanies each file.

Submission

By the time you submit your e-portfolio, you should have a complete package of files and folders, all clearly linked and accessed through a professional-looking homepage.

✦ You will have tested it on a number of different machines and asked others to test it for you.

✦ You will have incorporated the suggestions that the testers made to improve your work.

✦ You will have checked every link and removed any that do not work.

✦ You will have checked that your e-portfolio contains everything that you need it to contain.

✦ You will have checked the total file size and it is below the limit of 15 MB set by the awarding body.

✦ You have checked that every file opens quickly and displays as expected.

Now comes the time to submit your work.

Although your work may be submitted to the moderator electronically using a secure Internet link, it is likely that you will be asked to submit a separate copy to your teacher, so that they can take it away with them for marking.

You should decide on the most appropriate method of submitting your e-portfolio. There are a number of options.

Format	Capacity	Advantages	Disadvantages
CD	700MB	Plenty of space Cheap (less than 10p per CD) Easy to print labels	Need a CD writer Lots of wasted capacity Can get scratched
USB memory stick	Up to 2GB	Available in a variety of sizes Looks good Highly portable	Expensive (relative to CD) Difficult to label
Flash memory	Up to 2GB	Available in a variety of sizes Fast, easy to use	Expensive (relative to CD) Need card reader

Tip

Although there are no marks for this aspect of the presentation of your e-portfolio, it does add a feeling of professionalism to your work. Don't be afraid to make it look good.

You should check with your teacher to make sure that the format you choose is acceptable.

How do I get good marks?

✓ Your chances of getting good marks are improved if you complete your e-portfolio, it is easy to navigate and there are no hidden files.

✓ Make sure you have tested the portfolio and are confident anyone can find anything in it. Remember that you will not be with the examiner and you will not be able to explain where things are – everything should be self-explanatory.

Homework

1 Your homepage is very important – make sure it works well and is easy to follow. Try using two or three hyperlinks to some saved files and check that you can navigate to them.

2 Ensure that you have access to the appropriate file conversion applications.

3 Check the accessibility rules at www.w3.org.

4 Always test your work using other people. Sometimes you do not see an obvious problem because you have been working on a piece for too long. Marks will be awarded for testing and evaluation work.

CHAPTER 9

Project planning for enterprise

What you will learn in this chapter

In this chapter you will learn about the risks presented by not planning a project and how to avoid the common pitfalls of running a large project.

This chapter will describe how to manage a project as complex as a business proposal or a summative project brief (SPB). It will also explain why certain things should be considered at particular points in the development of your products.

Introduction

It will become very clear early on in your project whether or not your work has been planned and why it would have been a good idea! Project planning will help you to keep moving forward as you work. You will find you are not waiting for things or suddenly surprised by a problem that has loomed up. In industry, project planning is always done before a large project begins because it helps people decide what they need when, and who they need when. You will work more efficiently, you will be in control and you will be able to work to a set plan of actions.

The critical point will come when you send your DiDA SPB to the examiner. At this stage it should be finished and it must be no larger than the 15 MB specified. Huge files with voice and sounds, images and text may not ever get there. So file saving and file types need to be checked. Information on files is in an earlier chapter. If you have a number of tasks to fulfil, planning will allow you to set out how much time can be spent on each item that goes into your SPB.

Business SPB and planning

All units of the DiDA diploma are assessed via an SPB in which students bring together the knowledge, skills and understanding they have acquired throughout the unit into one substantial piece of work. This is marked by the teacher and externally moderated. Students usually complete the project toward the end of the course.

The project is a very important and sizeable piece of work, which must be done in school or college. The project is the only part of the course that is externally assessed and will be used to examine your skills in using ICT, planning and developing ideas to complete a finished product. It is recommended that a minimum of 30 hours should be allowed for this project.

Why bother planning?

Anyone who runs a successful business will say you plan to succeed. In business you usually plan ahead; for instance clothing is seasonal, so if no autumn ranges are ready at the start of autumn your business will simply fail. It is easier to work through a plan of your DiDA project than to jump from one unplanned action to another. Planning, if done well, should speed you along and give you clear aims and objectives, plus it helps you judge where you are in the whole project so you can maximise the marks you will be awarded. If you do not plan, you cannot work efficiently. You probably will be wasting time doing things that may not be in the right sequence and encounter hold-ups and risk having waiting time.

At the outset you will be given a set of intended objectives. You need to make sure that you clearly understand these objectives, as they will be used to assess how successful your enterprise product has been. You need to be totally confident that your project has a purpose. You need to know where you are going and for what reason.

Most of your products will have at least two purposes:

✦   to satisfy the client's needs;

✦   to help you to gain your DiDA qualification.

These two purposes should complement each other; the nearer you get to satisfying the client's needs, the nearer you will be to achieving the marks needed to get your DiDA qualification.

Professional project planners will often use specialist software to help them manage the tasks that together make up a project. Some of these applications may be available to you when you are working on your DiDA project.

✦ Microsoft® Project is an arrangement of spreadsheet, database, charting and text systems. If you have this application, it is worth taking a look at it as you may wish to use it for your work. However, it may take you a while to get to grips with it.

Task Name	Duration	Predecessors	8/11 Mo	8/12 Tu	8/13 We	8/14 Th	8/15 Fr	8/16 Sa	8/17 Su	8/18 Mo
T1	2 days									
T2	2 days	1,3								
T3	4 days									

Project management application

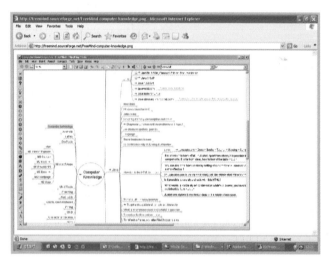

Mind-mapping application

✦ A slightly more straightforward system is mind mapping (mentioned earlier in the book). This is a system of noting everything you can think of that is related to the project (brainstorming) then adding details to each point. The different parts are then drawn together as a set of tasks that can be sequenced.

Both of these types of software are designed to help you manage your workload, but even if you decide to project-manage another way, say by using Microsoft Excel® or Microsoft® Word, you still need to meet the needs of your client – you need to develop a specification.

The specification

The specification could be:

✦ the definition of your DiDA project;

✦ a statement of the problems the brief has set you;

✦ *not the solution in itself – it is only the first step in what is sometimes a long journey!*

Before you start on the months of activity working on the DiDA project, you should write a specification. This is your definition of what is required and by when. There are not really any short cuts to this: if you fail to spend the time at the start, it will cost you far more later on.

A clearly written specification has a lot of benefits:

✦ The analysis of your problems will show up technical and practical details. This will cause you to read and think about the details of what you need to do.

✦ You will be able to set targets that can be checked along the way and used in your evaluation.

To enable you to successfully manage and develop a business project, you need to think about the following, as part of your specification:

✦ What or who is my product for?

✦ You need to be sure that you know why your product/final design is considered to be the correct outcome.

✦ Who is the target audience? You should have thought about age, gender, interests and other relevant information.

✦ What raw materials, components, applications and so on are required? Are they available to me?

✦ Do you know the technical requirements?

✦ You need to be sure you know of any limitations, such as sizes, costs or special considerations.

✦ Deadlines – all of them! Check what the timings of events will be before you start, and make a note of anything like holiday dates that may use up time in your time plan.

Milestones

If you underestimate the time involved for work and there are no timescales in your specification, you can assume that you will not finish on time and lose marks. Make yourself some 'milestones' (clear targets of what, by when). Stick them somewhere visible and tick them off as you progress.

Milestones help maintain progress and encourage effort. They allow you to judge how well you are doing and to celebrate progress throughout the project rather than just at its end.

The easiest way to make milestones is to use the timing information you have been given by your teacher or lecturer. They will know how long you have to complete the project. When you have worked out how long each subtask will take and have strung them together, you can identify the milestones for completing the tasks.

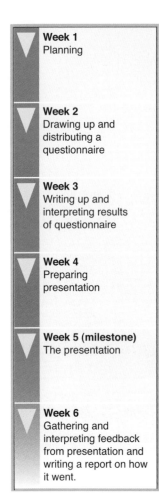

Week 1 Planning
Week 2 Drawing up and distributing a questionnaire
Week 3 Writing up and interpreting results of questionnaire
Week 4 Preparing presentation
Week 5 (milestone) The presentation
Week 6 Gathering and interpreting feedback from presentation and writing a report on how it went.

Timeline

Timeline

This is a linear (line) plan that you can use to plan what you want to achieve each week, month or even day. A timeline is a visual guide that will help you decide if everything is on time. Highlight points and milestones on the timeline and plan checks and feedback dates. Leave space on the timeline so that you can make notes or plan visits or meetings.

You will have several important stages in your project. You need to record your work at each stage then use this information to form your project evaluation.

Plan your activities

For DiDA make a list of all the tasks you need to do and allocate sufficient time to the tasks to match. Then list these tasks so that they are carried out in a sensible sequence. Think about what you can do right now and what you need to prepare for in order to work on other parts of your project. Make sure you don't reach the stage where you have nothing to do because you are waiting for something to arrive or something to happen – plan for it all.

Tip

Difficulties that may present themselves, as you work through your project, might have to do with resources not being available or extra tasks popping up during the course of the project. What often happens is your estimate of the time required to perform a certain task is incorrect – usually too short. Give yourself a little extra time – headroom.

Quality control

To save time some tasks can be grouped together. For instance some tasks, which are seemingly independent, may benefit from being done together since they may use common material or software. This would be common practice in most industries as it saves time and money. Think about the different parts of your project and see what could be done at the same time – for example scanning a batch of images for a range of products could be helpful.

Testing and quality

Your plan is not complete without clear provision for testing and quality. So each time you finish something, get it checked and ask for feedback from a friend or colleague. Try to get feedback from a range of people who you think can help improve your work or move it forward. Getting feedback, testing and checking things against their specifications can take longer than you think. So plan for it. If you are using experts you may need to phone, email or visit. This could cause delays.

Fighting for time

When working on DiDA you will be working on other things and in areas that have nothing to do with DiDA, so you need to balance the pressure and workload placed upon you. Once you have decided what you consider to be a sensible schedule, try to stick to it. If someone imposes an impossible deadline upon you which you cannot hope to meet, tell them and give your reasons. Your planning should include time where you stand back from the project and ask what can go wrong. Indeed, this is an excellent way of asking your classmates for their analysis of your plan.

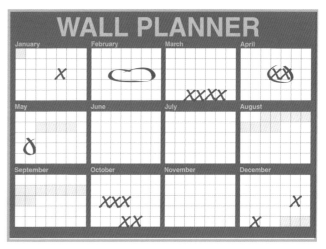

Calendar

Is it fit for purpose?

If you are keen, and take care in your work, you will probably do the best job possible. If you are really clear at the beginning of your project exactly what is needed, then you are probably more likely to be able to produce a successful business product.

To produce your work you will need to work with different types of software. Try not to learn how to use too many different types; this will take up valuable time and may not be necessary. You will need to select the software that fits your needs, and your skills and ability. Bear in mind that you can get similar results from many different applications. For instance Microsoft® Word can create websites, animations, posters, spreadsheets, forms and drawings.

Try to predict where the errors will occur. By examining the activities list you can usually pinpoint some which are risky, such as those involving new equipment, and those which are quite secure, such as those you have done often before. The problem areas might then be given a less fixed timescale – actually planning in time for the problems.

How do I get good marks?

✓ Refer back to your plan and your specification to see if you met their requirements.

✓ Evaluate your objectives – have you achieved them or not, and why (not just a checklist)?

✓ Always ask for feedback from others and document it so it is available to be examined.

✓ Always consider the whole process of your project from beginning to end.

✓ Make valid suggestions for improvements to your project and explain them.

✓ Always explain what you did and justify why you did it.

Homework

1 Produce a single page containing a thorough breakdown of the project you are working on. This should be presented in an easy-to-follow and interesting way. Add milestones.

2 Put together a timeline for an activity you are confident with, such as loading up and writing a letter in Microsoft® Word. Are there any activities that could be done while others are being carried out, such as switching on the printer, checking paper and so on?

3 Produce a template for an end-of-stage report. This should have space for:

Name
Candidate Number
Project title
Stage title
Date of start of project
Date of start of stage
Date of end of stage
Date of report
Comments
Comments from others

CHAPTER 10

Review and evaluation

What you will learn in this chapter

In this chapter you will learn about carrying out a review of your work, and how to use that review in evaluations.

When to review?

At the end of a project there should always be a formal evaluation or review. This should look back over the length of the project as well as examine the final outcomes.

However it is also important to review your work as it progresses so that you can adjust your plan or amend the allocation of resources to meet milestones and achieve a successful outcome.

Much of your work will be in the form of a project. The previous chapter went through the planning sequence you should follow. This chapter is concerned with how you can evaluate your work and use the results of the evaluation to better inform planning for future work.

Project management can be a very formal activity, and it often has a formal sequence of evaluating or reviewing work as it progresses. One part of the sequence is called a stage.

Each stage has a start, middle and end.

The start is characterised by the setting of the target – what you intend to achieve:

✦ Your business plan was the main starting point and sets the scene for the rest of your work.

The middle is where it actually gets done, the activity takes place:

✦ This is the running of your business – the work!

The end of a stage is where you can say, 'That is done, what's next?'

✦ This is the review point.

Following the plan

At the review point you need to look carefully at your business plan and ask yourself a number of questions:

Look carefully at your plan

✦ Is the plan being followed?

✦ Is the financial plan being achieved?

✦ Are the objectives being met?

Tip

Don't try to duck the issues – many companies that fail do so because the managers don't tackle important issues early enough.

If you put your plan together well, it will be easier to check that you are sticking to it. Take a look at these two plans – which do you think is the easiest to review and work with?

Plan 1

Over the first year we are hoping to build up a lot of customers. That will mean that we will make more profit at the end of the year than we will at the beginning. The increase in profit will pay off the loan that we will use for the start-up costs of the business.

Plan 2

We will need to borrow £1000 to start up the business. This will be used to buy stock and pay wages for the first month. At the end of the first month we expect to have £100 to reinvest from the sales. We expect to grow sales by £100 per month after the first month, so that by the end of the first year we will have paid off the loan and should be in profit by £200.

As you can see from these two plans the second company has confidence in its plan – it assumes that the company will be successful. It would be unlikely that anyone would embark on the development of a business if they were not confident of success.

Unfortunately confidence does not always mean it will be a success – there are lots of companies that are managed by people that are confident that they are going to do well, but that confidence is misplaced. Take a look on the Internet for the ENRON story. Thousands of investors were confident that everything was going well, because the bosses were saying everything was fine – but it wasn't!

What to review?

Earlier in this unit you were asked to develop a corporate look for your business. This needs to be regularly reviewed so that you can be confident that your customers or clients are aware of your company, but also so that new or potential customers know that you are a quality company.

Try running a search on the Internet for the history of the BBC logo – there are a few sites that have a record of the different logos that the BBC has used over its 70 years or so.

Why do you think the logos have changed? Sometimes it will have been because of changes in fashion, sometimes because the technology has improved and made it possible to make more innovative imagery. But sometimes it will have been because the message needed to change: what was being conveyed by the logo was not what the company wanted anymore.

In the early stages of the development of a business it will be important to keep the public face stable. Choose a logo or corporate feel and stick with it but build in a time for reviewing the logo, so that it does not become stale. The Matereality Ltd logo is a blue eye, but the website has been carrying a yellow development of this for some time, so that users start to link the two. Over time the blue eye is being phased out and the yellow eye is taking over.

It is also time to review the Learn2 logo and corporate look – take a look at the website (www.learn2.co.uk) and see if you could suggest some new ideas.

At the end of each stage you will need to carry out a range of reviews and build these into a log that you can refer to in your final evaluation. This log can help to influence developments and keep you on track as far as your business plan is concerned.

Review your logo

Carrying out an evaluation is about improving your work – you need to learn from your mistakes and congratulate yourself on your successes.

The evaluation methods you use and the questions you ask will depend upon your programme and your reasons for evaluating. There are many forms that a process of assessment can take, some more formal and others less so.

Collecting good information about your work will undoubtedly require more than one method. The shape that evaluation takes can depend upon:

✦ the questions you are trying to answer;

✦ the people or group you are trying to gather information from;

✦ the way in which you expect the results to be used.

The clearer you are on why you are evaluating and what questions you would like to answer, the better your results will be.

Your evaluation should not be something that you do on your own. It is extremely difficult to be objective about your own work – something you need to be if your evaluation is to be useful.

Always try to involve others. You may have seen short questionnaires in shops or restaurants that ask for comments about the service you have received from the staff. This is a simple method of collecting data, but more importantly it is being submitted by the end-user – the customer. This can be much more useful in reviewing the service that any number of managers or staff sitting down and writing an evaluation.

There are often 'user reviews' on websites. These usually take the form of a few simple questions that are completed and submitted through the website. The company can then use the data gathered to find out how effective its website has been.

You could develop a simple questionnaire for your customers that can be used to gather data that will inform your evaluation and further developments of your business plan. You should try to ask no more than ten questions and try to limit the potential answers by using multiple-choice type questions. This makes it a lot easier to collate the responses and use the data later.

More information on developing user surveys and carrying out research can be found in Book 1 of this series.

There are some aspect of your work that customers or end-users will find difficult to comment upon. These bits you will need to do for yourself and, as stated earlier, be honest; don't duck the questions or try to fudge the answers – it doesn't help in the long run.

Evaluating your work

Milestones

At the beginning of any project you will need to set milestones – and the review and evaluation points are when you need to state how well you are doing at meeting those milestones.

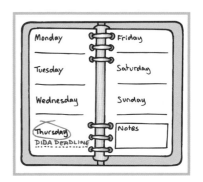

Review progress

In business, milestones or deadlines are immoveable – not like in school. If you are set a homework that has to be in on Monday and you don't give it in until Tuesday, you will possibly get told off, or have to suffer detention. But if you have to supply your tax return by a certain date and you miss it, you will have a fine to pay.

This is another reason for carrying out reviews throughout the project, rather than just at the end. If, as you are working through a particular stage, you realise that a milestone is approaching that you will not be able to meet, you can warn people.

If you are unable to deliver something to a customer on an agreed date, they will be much more understanding if you can let them know in advance, so that they can rearrange their schedules. If you don't let them know, they will be expecting the delivery and when it doesn't arrive they will be less able to make alternative arrangements, and therefore blame you for any inconvenience.

How well did you plan your work?

In responding to this, you need to think about the two plans at the start of this chapter. Did you put together a detailed and structured plan that can be used to help structure your work, or did you put together a vague and woolly plan with nothing definite in it?

If your plan was not very detailed and structured it will be difficult to say whether you have achieved your objectives. Remember the saying, 'If you don't know where you are going, you won't know when you've got there.'

Spending time at the beginning of the project putting together a detailed and well-structured plan will pay off later. Even if you fail to achieve some of your goals, you will at least be able to say why, and that can be invaluable in developing further work.

What went wrong?

In your review you should also record what went wrong, so that the same mistakes are not made later.

This includes recording why milestones were not met. Don't just blame someone else: think carefully about what happened to make you miss the milestone and record anything that you could have done to avoid it happening again.

If you were forced to miss a deadline because your supplier did not get the raw materials to you in time for you to manufacture an item, it may appear to be the supplier's fault. But could this have been avoided by you ordering the materials earlier, or having greater communication with your supplier?

If you try to blame someone else or try to avoid the truth, your evaluation will not be as good as one that is honest and not only admits where there have been problems, but also highlights where improvements could be made for future work.

Feedback from others

Try to include feedback from a range of other people, including your customers and clients.

Don't worry about people being negative when they give feedback – if it was all good you would find it very difficult to make improvements! The other thing to bear in mind is that they should be commenting on your work, not on you. So don't take things personally.

Ask a range of different people, or ask for feedback in different ways. Experiment with asking for feedback at different stages in your project: when you are just beginning a new stage, when you have completed a stage or when you think you are finished.

But remember to record the feedback for the assessor – this could be done as a summary of a set of questions or even as a video made up from a few people commenting to camera.

Final evaluation

You need to supply a final evaluation of your success in developing your business plan. This could be done in a variety of ways:

✦ written evaluation

✦ verbal evaluation, recorded in an appropriate manner

✦ presentation.

Each of these have their advantages and disadvantages. But whichever you choose, you need to make sure that you include everything that is mentioned above. The following checklist may help:

- What went well?

  – Why?

- What did not go well?

  – Why?

- Were the deadlines met?

  – Why?

- What could I have done better?

- Is there anything that I would change if I had to do it again?

- Feedback/comments from others.

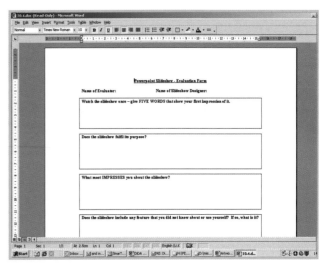

Evaluation presentation

Homework

1 Design a simple feedback form for your customers/clients that they could complete quickly and easily, which would give you some useful feedback.

2 Make a list of questions that you could ask your classmates that would help you to write a meaningful evaluation.

3 Produce a simple review of your logo or corporate look. State whether you think it needs to be redesigned or improved.

CHAPTER 11

Standard ways of working for enterprise

What you will learn in this chapter

This chapter will explain why you need to work in certain ways when following the DiDA qualification in ICT in Enterprise.

Rules and guidelines

Every business has its rules that must be followed. These rules are sometimes for safety, to protect people, and sometimes for security, to protect the business. Most of them are common sense and most people would agree they are a good idea. As we increasingly move from country to country for work, standard ways of working become even more important.

Enforcing rules

Official bodies enforce most of these rules; the police or even the army are used to enforce some. The fire brigade will enforce rules on fire safety and check out offices and factories fairly regularly. They will also offer advice. Her Majesty's Inspectorate (HMI) monitors others. However many rules are very difficult to enforce, or even to check to see they are being followed. There are too many businesses. Therefore guidelines are used.

Guidelines are recommendations; they describe methods of working. If these guidelines are followed they can help prevent accidents and make operations more efficient. Unfortunately there are rarely repercussions if the businesses fail to follow the guidelines.

Running across a busy road without looking would be silly as the chances of being knocked down would be high, you would be injured, medical time and cost would be involved and permanent injury would be a possibility. However using a zebra crossing to cross a road is a sensible idea and would be recommended. It would prevent injury, save distress for the driver of a car if they hit you, save worry for relatives, save money on medical costs and so on. Not to mention it may hurt! But you would not get arrested if you chose to ignore the advice and cross at another point further along the road.

Guidelines help prevent accidents

Without some sensible rules and guidelines all systems become chaotic – it's the same for ICT in business, enterprises and all industries.

Have you ever worked on a document, saved it and closed the application, only to come along sometime later and find that the file has disappeared? Usually people blame the computer or someone else, but it's almost certainly your fault. If the file had been named sensibly and filed in a suitable place that you could easily remember, it would have been easily found later.

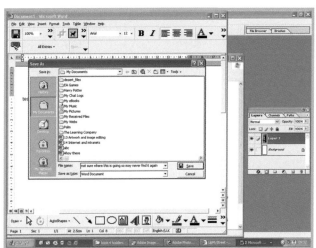

Sensible file naming

This chapter is all about working with ICT and enterprise projects in an organised and logical way, following simple and sensible rules, so that not only you and your own work improve, but everyone else is able to work safely and efficiently.

Before you start

Before embarking upon developing materials, you must ensure that your machine is safe and free of virus infection. A virus checker and a firewall usually protect a school machine, but as you may be sharing material between your home and school computer by sending files via email, you must ensure that your home machine is as safe too.

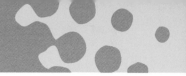

Virus checker

Effect of computer virus

Simply installing some anti-virus software is not good enough; you must make sure that it is up to date, it's on and that it stays updated automatically. This is the same for all security software.

Using ICT is still a relatively new field. Although computer systems date back to the Second World War, until the last twenty or so years very few people worked with computers on a daily basis.

This has meant that the ways of working in the industry are still evolving; new legislation and new procedures are developed, used and then amended, meaning that more new legislation and procedures need to be developed, and so on.

The way that ICT has grown has also led to a different approach to the way legislation is drafted and put into practice. There has to be much more international agreement to make the world safer for users as well as making international trade more efficient.

ICT is often seen as a way of making things faster, more efficient and more reliable. This can only be the case if everyone works in the same way – *a standard way of working.*

Speed and efficiency

One obvious advantage of using ICT to carry out certain tasks is the efficiency it brings. Modern processors can carry out billions of calculations per second, meaning that they can work incredibly quickly.

As you are developing your business ideas you will come to depend upon the speed of your machine. Many applications are very 'memory hungry' – they need lots of space to work in!

To make sure that your applications run smoothly, you should make sure that you do not have other programmes running in the background. For example, don't have a media player running while you are trying to convert video files into a particular format. Playing videos files from the Internet can seriously slow down your computer, so do not do so unless you have free time.

When you are using a new piece of software, try to get hold of the manual or the box; there will be a list of minimum requirements – your machine must exceed them. Your machine must have the minimum processor, memory capacity and processor speed. Software manufacturers always recommend a minimum specification for the computer to run their software, so if your machine is not up to it do not waste your time attempting to do the impossible.

Multiple applications

New processors have been developed that have onboard sound and graphics, and even dual processing, enabling billions of calculations to be carried out every second. Unfortunately, it is unlikely that the machines you have access to in school will be at this level of specification, hence the reason for not having other applications running in the background.

Unfortunately, just increasing the speed of an operation does not make it more efficient. Sports motorbikes are faster than most passenger cars, but they're not very good for getting away for a weekend in the summer with a family of four!

Application minimum requirements

So to make ICT more efficient, speed is only one aspect to be considered. Things such as reliability – how often a new computer breaks down, whether it has connections to all the necessary peripherals, whether the software is easy to use and so on are also factors which influence efficiency.

The way you use ICT is also a great influence over the efficiency of the system. Using the right application to carry out a task – such as Adobe Premiere® to edit video or Microsoft PowerPoint® for a slide-based presentation – helps to improve efficiency.

Speed isn't everything

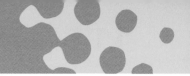

Legal requirements/sensible guidelines

There are also rules that you must follow, some of which are legal requirements such as the Data Protection Act and the Health and Safety at Work Act, and others are just sensible guidelines, such as taking regular breaks.

Your workspace

You should also consider the way in which you use the equipment and software, and the workspace that you operate within:

- Make sure that you have a safe environment to work in where there are no trailing wires or other obstructions.

- Position equipment away from direct sunlight.

- Position the screen so that your neck feels comfortable (a flat screen is usually the best type and should be anti-glare).

- Use well-designed furniture to help with posture and comfort.

- The desk height should enable you to reach the keyboard and mouse easily.

- Use wrist rests on mouse mats and keyboards.

- Position equipment so you can use it without twisting.

- Have suitable lighting without glare.

- Take regular breaks from the computer, every 20 minutes or so.

If these rules are not followed, using computers can lead to:

- backache

- eye strain and headaches

- RSI (repetitive strain injury)

- tiredness.

File management

Using a sensible method of filing is crucial. Everyone likes to work in their own way, but if people are working collaboratively – one of the advantages of using ICT – it is essential that everyone involved works together and uses a common approach to filing.

All ICT users must make sure that data used is accurate, consistent, reliable and stored securely.

The use of an appropriate file structure and naming convention can help to ensure that data is stored in a way that will allow easy and efficient retrieval. All applications record the date and time of a document's use; if the user also gives it a suitable name it should make it easier to find at a later date. Be aware that if you don't supply a name, applications can generate default names such as 'document1.doc' or 'sheet1.xls'.

The file type is also an important addition to a filename. Most operating systems have three-letter suffixes, or extensions, that denote the type of file. This is separated from the filename by a full stop; thus, '.doc' for a word-processed document or '.xls' for a spreadsheet.

Example

A video clip ripped from a camcorder could be called 'Birmingham bike show video.wmv'.

Although most systems can accept spaces, it is probably best to avoid them. The same goes for capital letters – use only lowercase – so the filename becomes 'birminghambikeshowvideo.wmv'.

As this can be a little confusing, the use of underscore '_' can take the place of the space, so the filename becomes 'birmingham_bike_show.wmv'.

As there may be more than one video from the show, or you may want to collect other videos, the use of a number can be advantageous, so the filename becomes 'birmingham_bike_show_01.wmv'.

Older systems prefer less than eight letters before the suffix, and it does make titles easier to remember if they have fewer characters, so the filename becomes 'b_bs_01.wmv'.

As long as everyone knows the system, anybody who needs to have access to the first bike show video from Birmingham should be able to find it. As long as nobody hits the wrong button!

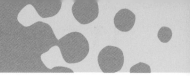

Careful folder structure design

Folder structure

Remembering filenames or the system used to generate them is one thing, but actually finding them is another. This is where the folder structure can be helpful.

Computer files can be stored in separate folders so that files of a similar nature can be grouped easily, for example:

◆ Images can be kept together in a folder named 'images'.

◆ Videos can be kept together in a folder named 'videos'.

The structure containing the folders should be carefully considered, such that navigating through to a particular file is a straightforward operation. This task is an essential element of developing your e-portfolio, as you need to make it as easy as possible for the marker to find each of your pieces.

It is also important that the files are stored in an appropriate format. Although Adobe Photoshop® is often used to manipulate graphical images, the format it uses to save images is only able to be read by Adobe applications. So if you were sharing an image it would be more appropriate and sensible to save it in a format that can be read by users who do not have access to Adobe Photoshop®, such as jpeg. This may mean the image loses some of its functionality, but that may not be as important as others being able to view the image.

As mentioned in other chapters, pdfs are a generic file type that can be read by most machines. So saving a file as pdf can mean that it is accessible by most people. However, unless they have specialist software, they will only be able to read the file, not amend it in any way.

Backups

It is good practice to take backups of your data. Many systems automatically back up data overnight; your school's management information system (MIS) will probably back up at least once a week, so that if anything happens the bulk of the data is safe.

Disaster recovery is big business. Companies that lose data through fire or theft can go bankrupt. Imagine the difficulty an international supplier would have if they lost all their sales records through someone pressing the wrong button! However, if backups and other systems are put in place, a lot of disasters can be avoided.

When a system starts to get used there are only a few files, but in time this could increase to many thousands – there were well over 500 files produced to write this book!

Many modern applications carry out an autosave every few minutes. This means that if anything happens, like a power cut or the battery running out on a laptop, your work is not completely lost! However, this is not something to rely upon. It is good practice to save your work regularly. I have saved this document twice in the last 5 minutes!

Sharing and security

If you work with others on a product, you may need to save different versions of files. If this is the case you can use the numbering system described previously – 'b_bs_01.wmv', 02, 03, 04 and so on.

It may also be advisable to set up a particular folder for shared material. If necessary the files and folder can also be protected by using passwords – check the help files of an application for guidance on how to do this for an individual file. For a folder you can use the operating system commands to share a folder over a network. Go to the Properties of the folder and select the Sharing tab. Depending upon your operating system, you should be able to share a folder openly with any other user, or privately with particular users. There are also help sites on the Internet that can offer independent security advice.

If your colleagues are further afield, you can share materials through online storage facilities. Again, these can be secured with passwords.

Bear in mind that any files that contain personal data fall under the Data Protection Act and you must therefore ensure that they are kept securely, and that access is limited to individuals that have been given express permission.

Remember that any system is only as secure as the people using it want it to be: a password is a great way of stopping people accessing materials they are not supposed to, but if the password is not kept secure the files won't be.

A similar thing is true with a credit card personal identification number (PIN); it only works if the user does not give their number to anyone else, or leave it for others to find.

If a folder has been set up to contain a number of files, it is sensible to list the contents of the folder with instructions on what each file is for. It is good practice to do this using a 'readme' file. The file is usually stored in a '.txt' format, so that it can be opened in a range of applications.

The readme.txt file usually has a simple description of what can be found in the folder and who to contact if there is a problem.

> **Readme.txt**
>
> In this folder there are 16 files:
>
> 4 jpeg images – these will open in any graphics package;
>
> 8 text documents (excluding this readme) – these are set to open in a text reader, they do not have any special formatting;
>
> 2 CSV files, these will open in a spreadsheet package;
>
> 1 short video clip, this should open in QuickTime®, you may have to download the latest version;
>
> and this readme file.
>
> If you have a problem opening any of the files, email me at dave@my_email.co.uk.

Software effectiveness

If you can remember when you first started using ICT, you may remember that everything took a lot longer – machines have not got that much better – you have.

Over the time you have used computers, you will have learnt some shortcuts such as using CTRL+C for copy and CTRL+V for paste, or using F1 for accessing the application help files.

Every software package has a vast array of helpful shortcuts that are easily found when you look at a menu item. The menu bar itself has an underline character in each title and the items on each menu also have one letter underlined. By pressing ALT and the letter in the title, the menu is expanded, and then to access the individual item, you need to press SHIFT and the underlined letter in the item.

> **Example**
>
> To show the Task Pane in a Microsoft® application:
>
> ALT+V followed by SHIFT+K

Some functions are common across applications, such as copy and paste, but some only work in particular pieces of software.

Applications such as Adobe Premiere®, not only have shortcuts on the menus, but the developers have made specialist keyboards, with coloured keys and other labelling. These keyboards can prove very useful if you intend to use such applications regularly.

You may have come across various computer mouse configurations: one button, three buttons, buttons and wheels, rollerballs, joysticks and all manner of other things to enable you to control movement on the screen. These each have their role; some are flexible and can be used in a general capacity, and others are designed to be good at a particular task or for controlling a particular application.

Shortcuts can also be used to access common functions. If you look at the icons on your desktop, you will see a number of shortcuts. When clicked they carry out a particular function, such as opening a folder or starting an application. They are very useful tools in speeding up how you use a computer.

Various keyboards and mice

Right-clicking on an item and choosing Create Shortcut creates a small file which can be cut and pasted to another location, but it will remember what it is a shortcut to.

Adding shortcuts within a filing system can also be useful, as the shortcut can connect the user to files which are stored elsewhere on the system without having to move or duplicate the files.

Quality frameworks

A lot of good practice is common sense. Most of what has been mentioned above is good practice. But to ensure that standards are raised it is important to work within a quality framework.

Tip

It helps if you can choose the correct tool for a job. In manufacturing the skilled worker is the one that is best able to select and use the appropriate tool. This is the same in ICT. Selecting the correct application and tools within an application will make you a much more efficient user of ICT.

Checking

With modern word processing and Desk Top Publishing (DTP) applications there is no excuse for poor spelling. Each software package has a spellchecker and most will also check grammar. Some systems have thesaurus and dictionary functions or even links to encyclopaedia entries. But even if the version you are working with does not have all this functionality, if you have access to the Internet, you can get help with any aspect of your work by accessing websites that can perform checks for you, such as dictionary.com.

> **Tip**
>
> Don't just copy chunks of data from encyclopaedia sites, the skill is in being able to adapt the material to your needs – copying is just plagiarism and easy to detect.

However, even with all of the help tools working and checks being run constantly, you still need to check materials for yourself. Proofreading is essential for all documents, not just text documents. You need to check that audio and video illustrate the right points, slide transitions all work when expected and so on.

If a document is to be printed you must also make sure that before printing you do a Print Preview. This should be done every time a file is updated, prior to printing. Remember a tree died for that piece of paper!

Earlier chapters also mentioned the need for getting other people to check your work, such as a sample audience. This can be a very useful tool, as you may not spot what other people find obvious – you may have spotted an error in this book that we never noticed.

Acknowledgements

You must also make sure that you recognise when others have helped you and acknowledge that in your work. This also goes for acknowledging any sources of information and authenticating your own work. You will be submitting an e-portfolio for assessment that will have to be authenticated, proving that the work within it is yours. However you must also point out where and how you have been helped.

By authenticating your work, you are stating that you have worked with Standard Ways of Working, and in doing so have complied with all appropriate rules and regulations; you have acknowledged where you have used other people's work or ideas and sought and received help. You have also ensured that material that is confidential has been kept secure and only those with particular reason have had access to it.

As mentioned above there are certain laws and guides that you also need to work within. The Data Protection Act is most often mentioned where ICT is concerned, but there are other laws that you need to be aware of.

The Data Protection Act (DPA)	Controls how personal data is handled and distributed. Essential reading for anyone dealing with personal data.
The Health and Safety at Work Act	Covers health and safety in the workplace, this ensures that accidents are minimised. Just because you don't work there doesn't mean it's not a workplace! Other people do.
The Disability Discrimination Act (DDA)	Related to access for all, ensuring that people are not disadvantaged through physical disability or learning difficulty.
The Special Educational Needs Discrimination Act (SENDA)	Linked to the DDA, but more specifically for those with learning difficulties.
Copyright and Patents legislation	Covers all published materials and manufactured goods. If something is used for gain, it must be credited, and in most cases paid for.

Homework

1 Carry out an audit of your workspace. What can be done to improve it?

    a. Produce a simple business plan, highlighting some of the problems faced by computer users and the work involved in remedying the main issues, such as:

        i. poor lighting

        ii. poor equipment lights and lack of adjustment on furniture

        iii. poor storage space.

2 Use the Internet to find out about the laws covering copyright of images and sound.

    a. Produce a page, explaining:

        i. what can be done legally;

        ii. what you should avoid doing;

        iii. what must not be done;

        iv. who is responsible.

3 Produce a set of rules that could be used as the basis of a contract between you and your tutor to ensure that you worked safely and efficiently.

CHAPTER 12

Artwork and image-editing software

What you will learn in this chapter

You will learn about image-editing software, the names of tools common to this type of software and how to create exciting text and images. You will also learn how to download free image-editing software that will cover all the needs for your course if you cannot use Adobe Photoshop® to manipulate images. There is a general skills section that should get you started with this type of software.

Tools

Image-editing software is any piece of software that can change an image.

You will find tools to do just this in a basic way in Microsoft® Word, Xara and Picasa™ (Picasa can be found in Google™ and is free). Most people have access to Microsoft® Word so can at least prepare their images in a simple way.

At the other end of the spectrum are Adobe Photoshop® and Corel® Photo-Paint. Adobe Photoshop® is used by professional designers throughout the world and is designed for altering images. You can however use Adobe Photoshop® to paint, create unusual text and prepare work for the web. Adobe Photoshop® usually comes with image-ready software, which is specially designed for web design and animating objects.

In industry, when producing artwork you would use Adobe Photoshop® for changing your images or a similar image manipulation package, such as Adobe Illustrator® or CorelDRAW®. You would use a similar graphics packages for working on typography, images and colour. To create the pages for a publication, a desktop-publishing package such as Microsoft® Publisher, Adobe PageMaker® or QuarkXPress® would be used by adding files from the two types of software we have just mentioned. For web authoring and design you may use a combination of the above plus specific web design software. Most of the software mentioned is used by designers and printing businesses throughout the world; they are industry standard packages.

They can however be used at different levels. Adobe Photoshop® for instance comes in two packs: one is a lot cheaper to buy than the other, but both will do all you need for DiDA. Adobe Photoshop Elements® is a cut-down version of Adobe Photoshop® which will more than cover all the needs of most home and education users and is a fraction of the cost of the full-blown version.

Image editing

The images produced by scanners and digital cameras are often OK but not usually good enough to use in publicity materials. If your aim is to make images that are outstanding or creative you will need to edit them.

Image editing is used to transform a snapshot or scanned image into a work of art. Many of our printers are good quality but often what we see on paper is disappointing. An image editor can make up for these failings and create an enhanced version of your image ready for presentation.

Some of the basic aims of image editing are to:

✦ crop, rotate, correct perspective distortion and so on;

✦ remove dirty parts, dust, dots and scratches;

✦ adjust the brightness, contrast, colour tint and colour saturation either selectively or in total;

✦ sharpen the image or change the lighting.

More advanced uses of image-editing software are to:

✦ change colours;

✦ move selected parts of an image;

✦ add effects;

✦ produce amazing typography (letters);

✦ paint or draw;

✦ using the effects option, create brilliant designs.

Most image-editing software would be used for preparing images ready to be printed or sent to web pages as artwork, the main function of this kind of software. It is part of your creative toolbox.

Capturing images to your computer

You can capture images in many ways:

- ✦ scanners
- ✦ cameras
- ✦ dragging off the Internet
- ✦ you can buy images from image libraries (expensive)
- ✦ clip-art libraries.

There are two types of scanner you are likely to come across. The most common is the flat-bed scanner.

Tip

Size

One of the most important things to remember is that images created with software such as Adobe Photoshop® can be very large and thus often slow down your computer or keep crashing it. Always check the image size by going to Image at the top of the screen then Image Size and resize it smaller if it's too big. Adobe Photoshop® also allows you to check how big the file is by going to the bottom left-hand side of the screen. Along the margin is the file size.

Flat-bed scanner

With this machine you lay a book or page on the glass bed face down and the machine optically scans across the page, converts it to an image and delivers it to the scan software on your computer. This type of scanner is ideal for thick originals or larger pages.

Printer/scanner

The other type, the printer/scanner, is usually incorporated into a printer and is fed through the same as you would when printing. These machines are useful because you do not have to buy a separate scanner so they take up less space. Of course you can only pass

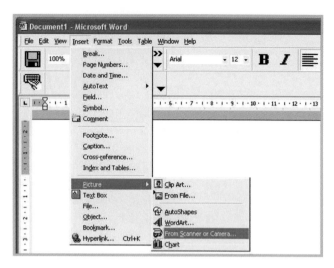

Inserting an image from a scanner into Microsoft®
Word

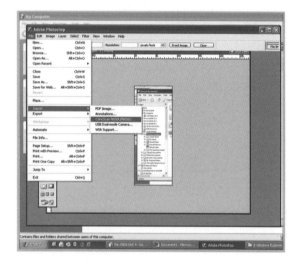

Importing an image from a scanner into Adobe Photoshop®

through thin paper or card that is no larger than the paper size the printer can take, usually A4.

Most scanning software allows you to do a prescan. A prescan scans the whole bed then allows you to make decisions on size or cropping and resolution. Resolution of 300dpi (dots per inch) is usually fine for print; for Internet images it can be less. The higher the resolution the more space it will take up in your computer's memory. You can set your scanner to work directly from Microsoft® Word.

Or you can scan directly into your image-editing software such as Adobe Photoshop®.

Tip

The tools palette in software such as Adobe Photoshop® and similar programs can be very extensive. Because of this, many of the tools and palettes are hidden until needed. In Adobe Photoshop® these toolbars have tiny arrowheads that reveal further tools when clicked. This is a common feature which saves the screen from cluttering up with dialogue boxes.

Techniques

Most image-editing software is based on processes that years ago were done in a darkroom with wet papers and chemicals. The finishing processes such as airbrushing and spotting out, retouching and adding effects can now be done on screen instead of in a darkroom.

Resizing

Zooming in and out of your images using the magnifying tool or the navigator tool does not alter the physical size of the image (the size it will print out). To change the size either to save memory or to get the image size right you can either use the Transform option which is under the Edit option, which allows you to scale the image manually, or resize using the Image Resize option, which allows you to scale the image down precisely to the size you require. I usually do this in centimetres but you can also use percentages.

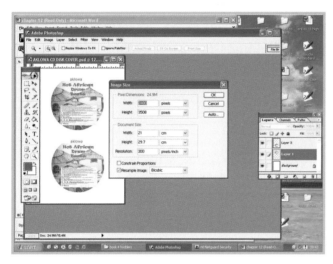

Retain proportions

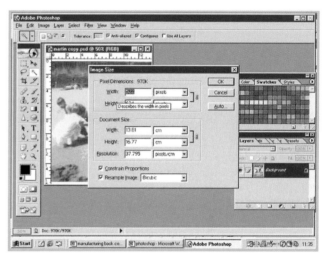

Image size proportions

Text

Adobe Photoshop® is not just about editing images. You can produce some really amazing typestyles using the layer effects option to create type that is embossed or has coloured edges, or text that takes up shapes. Text effects created with image-editing software can look stunning and are really easy to do. Possibly the easiest way to have fun with text is to apply effects. These can be controlled with sliders and can make relatively dull-looking headlines really interesting. The text effect can be used successfully on text for the screen, a part of a website or on printed material.

Text can also have shadows or drop shadows applied from the layer option. This process looks good especially on titles and headlines. Do not forget of course that you can apply all

Text before and after effects applied

the power of an image-editing package to any of your hand-drawn artwork or images by scanning the work directly into the software. In fact you can apply the power of scanning to leaves, twigs, shells, peel, bark, stones, flowers and so on – these all scan surprisingly well. You must of course be careful with the glass base to the scanner and refrain from looking at the light as it passes over the scanning bed.

Image-manipulation software is used by graphic designers, web designers, fashion designers and artists. Many people are surprised by the fact that artists use Adobe Photoshop®, but interestingly the package has most of the tools an art studio would have – brushes of all sizes and shapes, airbrushes, huge ranges of colours, light and dark options in the effects-render-lighting options and textures.

Hard or soft edges

Soft edges are usually more useful as they can blend each brush stroke and look more realistic. The selection tools can be used the same as brushes with hard edges or with soft edges. When you click on any selection tool an option appears on the top of your screen called 'feathering' which allows you to have soft edges. What you have to do is select the feathering value before you select anything on the image you are working on. The feathering option is based in pixels and allows for a fade to transparency. The need for a soft edge on selection tools becomes more obvious when you cut out an image and paste it onto a background – the image looks naturally in place. It's a bit likes the difference between cutting out with scissors or airbrushing an edge onto something: one is hard and sharp the other is soft. Feathering can also create a great effect on an image placed into text. The effects of feathering edges can be seen in many magazines and newspapers and is a very popular tool with graphics designers.

One of the most useful selection tools, which once again can be used with or without feathering, is the magic wand.

Feathered image

Magic wand icon

When selected, this tool has a tolerance. Instead of drawing around a part of your image, it seeks out similar colours or tones to the pixel you have clicked into. For instance if you had a very blue sky and needed to change the brightness or remove the blue and put on grey, the magic wand will seek out all the blue and allow you to delete or work on the blue areas. The tolerance level helps it to decide how much blue or how little you wish to remove. A low tolerance will mean it seeks very similar colours to the spot you first click into; a higher tolerance means it is less fussy and will seek general blues or whatever colour you click on. The magic wand is available in many graphics packages and is designed to help speed up work by automatically seeking the colours or tone you wish to work with.

Tip

Selection tools always show you what you have selected by putting marching ants around the selected area; marching ants are the little dots that move around the selected area.

Magic wand selection

Zooming

Eyestrain is a very important issue with any screen-based software so rather than use the magnifying glass try to use the navigator tool, which you should set up as soon as the software is loaded.

Navigation tools allow you to zoom in and out quickly and to move around a zoomed image fast. There is little point is straining your eyes looking at a tiny images when you can easily zoom in and out with this tool.

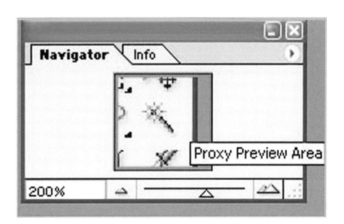

Navigation tool

Layers

Most graphics software has a layers option and for DiDA it is important you understand how these work. Layers are a bit like glass sheets that separate different images: each time you add a layer you create a separate glass sheet to work on. Just as you cannot paint through glass, the image you are working on cannot affect the image below.

TASK: Load up the Layers dialogue box.

On the background layer paint some brush strokes using a bold brush.

Put in a new layer by clicking in the New Layer option

Brush over this layer covering the layer with paint. Now get a rubber from the toolbox and rub out some of this brushwork to reveal the layer below.

In Adobe Photoshop® you can add many layers and link layers using the Chain icon; this will link changes such as transformation and position on the layer.

Tip

The best way to learn how to use layers is to cut and paste a few images onto a set of layers and either rub away part of each image or use the transparency option in the layers dialogue box to fade one layer into the other.

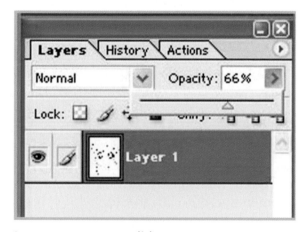

Layer transparency slider

Transform

The Transform option allows you to scale, flip, rotate or distort your image or text and create perspective. In Adobe Photoshop® you are given handles to pull or stretch your image. Handles normally appear on any object that can be resized. This includes image and text boxes in Microsoft® Word and most other software.

Handles to resize your image

You can scale your image up by putting in a number greater than 100 or down by choosing a number between 1 and 100. Make sure Constrain Proportions and Resample Image are selected (this is a little tick box in the bottom left-hand corner) otherwise your image will grow or shrink differently in each dimension, skewing the scale. If you wish to increase the resolution for better printing quality, while decreasing the overall image size, uncheck Resample Image.

Resolution should always be set to 72 pixels/inch so that the new graphic will work with common monitor resolutions. To make the changes to your document, click OK . To change the canvas size (your working area rather than the size of your image) by either adding additional space to the image or clipping space off the image, select Image > Canvas Size . By default, Adobe Photoshop® will add canvas in the background colour that has been selected. You can add (or delete) width, height or both.

Filters

To apply an effect to an image, select the parts you wish to add the filter to and choose the filter from the menu. There are a whole range of effects including artistic effects and textured effects. There are also hundreds of other filters that you can download free from the Internet, but most of them do similar operations. So think about the effect you want to convey to your audience.

Drawing

The drawing tools in Adobe Photoshop® are pencils, airbrushes and brushes. You can select the size of the pencil or brush by clicking on Brushes from the Window menu.

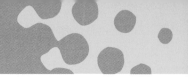

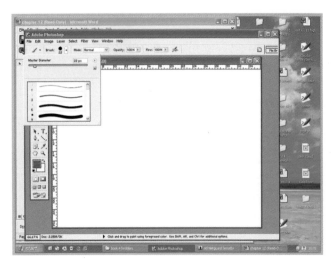

Select a brush

This will reveal the brushes, which can be sized with the slider or by clicking on preset sizes and shapes. As with filters, there are thousands of brushes available on the Internet and you probably have several on your machine.

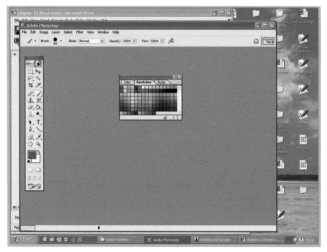

Colours and swatches

You move the brush around with your mouse, choosing to paint by clicking the right mouse key. If you have access to a drawing palette you can also experiment with using a stylus – these usually give much greater control over the use of the brush and will allow you to vary the pressure and the effect the brush has on the screen in the same way using a normal brush does.

The colours can be dipped into by going to the Window menu and selecting Colour or Swatches to reveal standard ink colours that are used by printers; there are usually hundreds of these available.

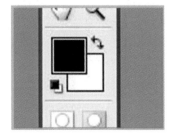

Foreground and background colours

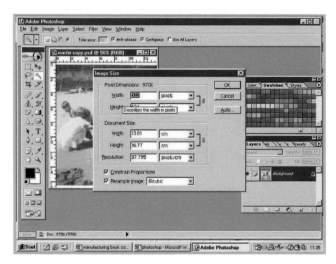

Image size

Grouping and ungrouping objects

Grouping can be done in most Microsoft® packages and just about every graphics package. Grouping is very useful because it allows you to work on several objects at once. To select objects for grouping, you can either select the first object, hold down the SHIFT key and click to select the others, or drag a marquee over the objects you want to group.

When you use the Group command in Microsoft® Word under Draw on the Drawing toolbar to group objects (a table, chart, graphic, equation or other form of information) they become bonded together. You can work with them as though they were a single object. You can flip, rotate, resize or scale all objects in a group as a single unit. You can Ungroup a group of objects at any time and then Regroup them later.

TASK: Flip or reverse a shape

Select a shape.

On the Shape menu, point to Rotate or Flip, and then click Flip Vertical or Flip Horizontal.

To switch the begin and end points on a line, on the Shape menu point to Operations and then click Reverse Ends.

How do I get good marks?

✓ Image manipulation is nearly always necessary when producing artwork (the final example of an image) so you need to show you have considered this when working with images. This type of software is probably the most powerfull you will use. So try to use it well.

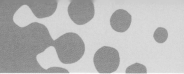

HOMEWORK

1 Go to a computer with a scanner. Put in a sharp image and scan into Adobe Photoshop® or similar software. Have a go at editing it. For instance you could go to the Tools section and place parts of the image in crazy positions, or try a range of effects.

2 Picasa™ (http://picasa.google.com/index.html) is free image-editing software that helps you edit and share all the pictures on your PC. Every time you open Picasa™, it automatically locates all your pictures (even those you forgot you had) and sorts out a visual album organised by date with folder names you will recognise. Start to make a photo resource for your DiDA work of images that may be useful. Make sure they are either your own or copyright free.

CHAPTER 13

Email

Introduction

Email has revolutionised the way we communicate with each other. As letter writing was dying out emails breathed fresh air into the art of communication with parents, friends and family throughout the world. Businesses embraced the idea quickly and now many use email as their primary source of communication. People can send and receive information in seconds. Email can also be used to send text, movies, instructions for machines' codes and news. Emails can be sent via computers, TVs or mobile phones. Email messaging has now become part of many people's lives.

The advantages of using email is that you can send information almost instantly anywhere. It has changed where and how businesses operate and it could be argued is good for the environment because you do not need to use paper, post or delivery companies. Work can be confidential and you can pick your emails up 24/7. With email people who once had to travel to work can communicate securely from home and pick up orders via the Internet from throughout the world.

What is email?

Email is an application that is used to send text, images, music, movies or any other type of file to anyone, anywhere around the world. You can only send emails to a person who has an email address.

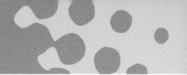

Email addresses usually look like this:

They have a **name**, an @ and the **name of the service provider** for example

A very common way of starting to use email is by subscribing to a free email service such as is MSN Hotmail® or Google Gmail™. If you follow the online form you can soon start to send emails and pick them up from a computer anywhere in the world. To do this you need to find the right web page for getting your emails and sign in using a password.

There are dozens of Internet service providers who make money from providing a free email service. They use the service as a means to send adverts or encourage you to use their more advanced, chargeable services.

Email is environmentally friendly – no petrol for the post office, no paper, no card, no stamps, no airmail. Email saves money – no phone-call charges, no postage and no energy to deliver the information other than the power on your PC, and it is quick. You can locate specialists and send and receive information or images relevant to your DiDA course. The negative side is that it can be used for criminal activities, and can easily be misunderstood (see later section on netiquette).

Viruses in email

One of the most common ways of introducing viruses into your computer or network is by opening attachments that have been sent without checking them first. It's too late once you've opened an attachment that contains a virus – it's already started and there is very little you can do about it, unless you have up-to-date virus protection. The people that send viruses in emails often try to trick users by stating the attachment is:

Information requested
As asked for
From Mr Smith (or some other name)

If in doubt delete it.

Using email

Microsoft® Outlook Express is email software that comes with the Windows® operating system and is one of the most common programs of this type. It lets you receive, send or save emails and has other facilities such as a spellchecker and formatting option.

Here are some of the things you can do with email:

Microsoft® Outlook Express

Write emails

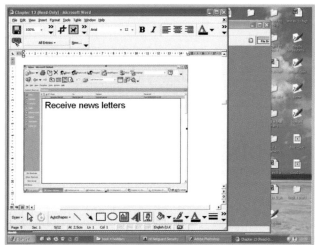

Receive emails

The following are some of the most commonly used free email providers. You can get to any of these by searching on their names on the Internet. Once you have reached the site you simply follow the simple instructions to set up your own email account.

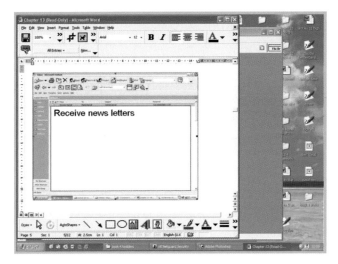

Attach files to your email

Email addresses need to be typed out *exactly* – if there are any errors the email cannot be sent. Even one error will mean it will not send.

Google Gmail™

Gmail™ is Google's email. It provides practically unlimited online storage that grows with your use. It allows you to collect all your messages in one place and access them from any machine, as it stores everything online. As you have a huge amount of free space, it is unlikely that you would ever need to delete an email.

Lycos® Mail

Lycos® Mail gives you junk or **spam** protection. This is very useful, as there are many emails that fall into this category and your mailbox can get overwhelmed if not protected.

MSN® Hotmail®

Hotmail® is one of the oldest free email providers and is used by millions of account holders. As with Gmail™, it stores everything online, so that the emails can be accessed from anywhere.

Yahoo!® Mail

Yahoo!® Mail is a reliable and secure email service with a good amount of storage and good spam filter to keep the junk out.

Email problems

Considering the many millions of people who use email, it is very reliable and rarely do messages go astray. Sometime the email servers have problems – these are the machines that collect and send emails to the various other servers around the world. But this is usually a temporary problem and soon put right.

Spam is junk email that fills up your inbox with emails you don't want. You can block these, but the best way to avoid spam is not getting on spammers' lists in the first place. Watch what you visit on the web, don't give out your email by filling in forms for competitions or free gifts and never open messages if you do not recognise the sender.

Sometimes when you sign up for something on the Internet, there is some innocent-looking text at the end of the form saying: 'YES, I want to be contacted by selected third parties.' Quite often, the tick box next to that text is already checked and your email address will be given to the spammers.

Email netiquette

If you write emails bear in mind the term 'netiquette'. This is a code of conduct that helps make sure emails are understood and not misinterpreted.

Because emails do not carry a smile or a laugh the person receiving it can interpret the message in the wrong way and become offended. You need to consider if the reader will understand what you mean from only the text.

Netiquette rules are:

✦ Making a joke in emails could be misinterpreted as bad news.

✦ Don't send an email you would not like to receive.

✦ Make sure your email is clear and easy to understand.

✦ Use information from the original message in your reply.

✦ Remember that not everyone is on broadband so huge files containing sounds, pictures or movies could hold up their machines for ages.

✦ Sarcasm never works in emails.

✦ Writing rude notes to people on emails always increases negativity.

✦ Sometime it's a good idea to share emails with others for sound reasons; forwarding is the answer. Click on forward and type in their address.

✦ Acrobat files confuse some people. Only use them if you know the receiver will understand what they are.

✦ The same with zipped files. Not everyone knows how to unzip.

✦ Capitals or bolds can be interpreted as shouting – try to avoid these.

Email safety

Although email is generally safe you need to use your common sense. A new email from someone you do not know may be from a boy or girl or long-lost relative, but it could be from a lunatic! Look in the newspaper and see how many people go wrong by following through with meetings via emails. So never give names, addresses or phone numbers out, never agree to meet someone and never give out personal information. If you do get a pest, use the email application's blocking system to refuse to accept emails from that address. If the worst comes to the worst change your address and tell only those you know you can trust.

If you find that someone is breaking the netiquette rules above, and using threatening or rude language, tell your email account company. They will investigate it and may involve the police.

When you sign up with an Internet service provider, they may include your first and last name in your email address. Most people don't even realise that their full name is being sent out with every email. This may be fine for businesses but it may present a security risk for you. Find out if you are giving out your name and how to change it.

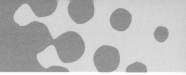

Bear in mind that banks and other financial institutions never send details by email – if they don't trust it, you shouldn't!

Look and see what name appears in the 'from box' when you send an email. Do you want a stranger having that much information about you? If someone knows your first and last name and the country that you live in, they could come knocking on your door.

Emails are wonderful to get, they keep you in touch and help share information, they link friends and help with work, but you need to use your common sense.

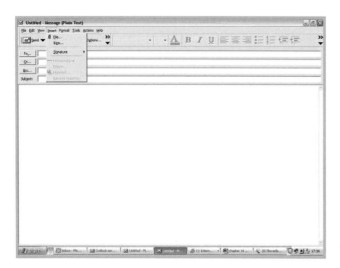

Microsoft® Outlook®

Signing up for an email account

It is important you check with your teachers and parents or carers about email rules and safety procedures before signing up. Many educational establishments have strict safety codes regarding email safety.

Hotmail® from MSN® is quick and easy to sign up for and can be accessed anywhere in the world.

With Hotmail® you simply go to their homepage, click the blue box and follow the instructions. If you have a very popular name you may need to add a number or short word after it in order to have that name. For instance when the sign-up page asks for your name and you type in 'Jsmith' you probably will find it is already allocated to someone, but 'jsmithiscool' may still be free. Therefore, your email address would become jsmithiscool@hotmail.com.

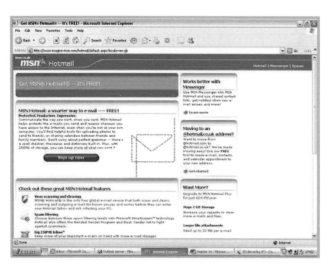

Creating your Hotmail® email address

Homework

1 Log into an email service provider's website and sign up for an email address. Most school and college students should have a school one at least. When you have subscribed, send yourself an email and see how long it takes to arrive. Check with your carers that this is OK to do. Make sure you follow the codes for safety issued by your establishment.

2 Type your name into a web browser and see what comes up – you may be surprised!

3 Look at the storage that different email providers offer and list which gives you the most space.

Internet and intranets for enterprise

What you will learn in this chapter

In this chapter you will learn how the Internet came about and how to use it efficiently. There is a lot of jargon associated with the Internet and some of this is explained.

The Internet

If you imagine the Internet as a huge network of computers spread around the world with servers in many countries, that's a pretty accurate description. In fact it is a huge network of networks. Every computer that logs on to the Internet does so through some sort of provider (NTL, BT, MSN®) – this gateway is the link from one network to all the others. Once the door is opened you can access millions of sites from anywhere in the world. There is information, good and bad news, games, music, videos and messaging going on from one side of the world to the other.

The Internet began shortly after the Second World War, when a group of scientists who had been working together during the war decided to keep in touch and continue to work collaboratively. This small group worked in different institutions, mostly in the USA, and they linked the primitive computer systems of their workplaces together over the normal telephone system. There was no broadband or satellite connection in those days.

Sixty years later there are millions of businesses and people using the Internet! Businesses depend on the Internet now for running their information across the world, checking data and computing it, communicating by video links, selling their products and controlling equipment and machines.

Intranets

Intranets are like mini Internets, often set up and used by a single organisation. Individuals within the organisation can log on to them but they are not available to the general public. Intranet systems are basically closed networks that run exactly as the Internet does. To a user there is rarely any noticeable difference in the way an intranet system functions compared to the Internet. An oil company for example could use their intranet to link up with their bases in other countries and include company software, trading details, confidential news, information on human resources, health and safety, crisis management, training and market reports. It may link to home users who can log on to the intranet to do their work.

Sometimes an intranet system is confined to a geographical area, such as a town, and it is kept within a company premises. There are a number of intranets that can be accessed from anywhere, but they usually require the user to have a password to log in.

Intranets are really useful where private and confidential material needs to be transferred over a network or users needs to be monitored, as in a school network. To use the example of the road system, a closed road system is a good place to test a new car, where the public won't be able to see it; it is also a good place to check how often a driver exceeds the speed limit!

Most schools and most large organisations have intranets, and some have developed extranets – a word that has recently come to mean an intranet system that can be accessed remotely over the Internet but requires a password to gain entrance.

The World Wide Web

The World Wide Web (WWW) is the most commonly used part of the Internet. This is the system that contains linked images, text, sound, video, information to run CADCAM machines, remotely check weather, links to web cams for live information about anything anywhere and deliver them anywhere in the world to any suitable computer.

There are other systems that transmit data over the Internet – email for example – that are not part of the WWW.

In order to have access to this massive resource, the computers have to have a common language to create and link resources. The language most commonly used is Hypertext Mark-up Language or HTML. It uses a variety of words and instructions to communicate across the Internet.

There are other languages used to display information received from the Internet, such as Java™, Lingo and some others, but these are usually delivered by an HTML page: a bit like a jam doughnut – the jam comes inside the doughnut. Although the two materials are completely different it would be very difficult to transport the jam without the doughnut (some might add that the doughnut is the dull bit, and the jam the bit that's more fun – to continue the analogy!)

To view the programming language that a web page has been built in, in your web browser click on View, Source (ALT+V, SHIFT+C).

Browsers

For a computer to be able to understand any of these languages it must have an application installed that can decode the data – a 'browser'.

Broadband modem

A browser can come in a variety of types: by far the most common is Microsoft Internet Explorer®, an application developed as part of the Windows® system. But there are others: for PCs Mozilla Firefox® and Opera are becoming more popular; AOL users have their own system.

Whichever system is used, the principle is the same – the electronic data stream transmitted over the Internet is decoded via a modem into a programming language, HTML, and passed to the browser application.

The browser is able to translate the HTML into a page that can be shown on the screen for the user to view.

Firefox plug-ins

Modern browsers are able to handle a wide variety of file types and media, through the addition of 'plug-ins' or 'add-ons'. These are small bits of programs that are added to the browser application. You could think of them as foreign-language dictionaries. The browser uses the plug-in to translate the code of a particular file type, as a person could use a foreign-language dictionary to translate a word or sentence.

Addresses

To be able to access information over the Internet you need to know where it is.

If you walk into a library and ask the librarian for 'a book' you will probably be laughed at! If you were to ask for a book about dinosaurs, you could be directed to a range of books, but it would be even better if you asked for a particular book, by a particular author.

If you want a precise piece of information you need to be able to ask a direct and accurate question – 'Could you tell me, what is the third word on the fifth line of the last page of Romeo and Juliet, please?'

The librarian can then provide exactly what you require.

Learn2 website

The Internet is just like a massive library – it has pages covering every subject you can imagine, from Aardvarks to Zebras and everything in-between!

To make sure you have a fruitful time on the Internet you must be prepared. Make sure you know what you want or where you can find it.

Websites all have addresses – Uniform Resource Locators (URLs). These are like household addresses, and they are made up from particular strings of data. If you can understand how they are made up, you stand a better chance of using them efficiently.

Take the address http://www.learn2.co.uk/dida

This is made from a number of elements:

✦ http:// stands for hypertext transfer protocol – this is the system used by the Internet to let the browser know that it will be receiving hypertext pages.

✦ www. This is the address of the web server that holds the web page. It's usually www, but it doesn't have to be.

✦ learn2. This is part of the 'domain name'. It is usually a name that has been purchased and registered by someone, a company or an organisation.

◆ co.uk This is a suffix available for companies based in the UK. There are lots of others; .com is the most common as it relates to companies that can be based anywhere. Gov.uk is the suffix used by sites that are government run, ac.uk is for colleges, sch.uk is for schools and so on.

◆ /dida This slash followed by a name, directs the web server to look in its subdirectory named 'dida'.

The web server will automatically follow the direction given by the URL and then look for a page with the title index or home, usually with a file type suffix of htm (abbreviated from HTML).

If it finds a page with the correct name, it will then grab the data and return it to the browser. On receipt, the browser will translate the code and rebuild the web page as it was designed to look.

If the URL contains an error then either the web server will not respond or it will not be able to find the correct page and the browser will not be able to show the expected result.

Browser controls

As with all applications a browser has a graphical user interface (GUI) that is designed to make most of the operations straightforward to carry out, usually with only a few clicks of the mouse.

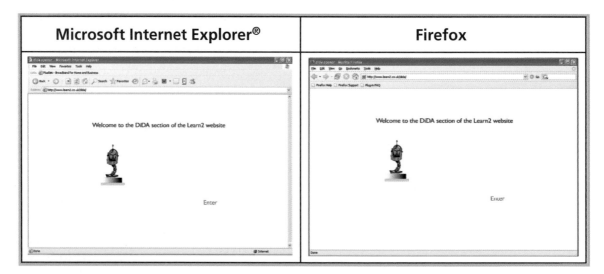

Browser similarities

Both Microsoft Internet Explorer® and Firefox have almost identical functions.

14 Internet and intranets for enterprise

The title bar at the top of the browser window gives the title of the page you are viewing and contains the Minimise, Maximise and Close buttons.

The menu bar contains File, Edit, View, Tools and Help links. There are also links to what Microsoft Internet Explorer® calls 'Favorites' (note the American spelling) and Firefox and other browsers call 'Bookmarks'; these are the same thing – they are URLs recorded in the browser memory, for future reference.

Most of the menu commands are the same across the different browsers, as they are designed to do the same job – display web pages.

The buttons on the toolbars also carry out the same operations, although they may look slightly different.

Microsoft Internet Explorer®	Firefox	Description
Back		Back – return to the page you viewed immediately prior to the one showing in the browser.
		Forward – go forward to the page you have just gone 'back' from.
		Stop – stop whatever is happening; useful if you have clicked something by mistake.
		Refresh – pages can be loaded incorrectly, or information can be updated without the browser getting the updates; by clicking refresh a request is sent to the web server to get the latest version of the page.
		Home – this is the page that is shown when the browser starts – the home page. It can be set to any URL, but usually starts as something to do with the browser or the Internet Service Provider (ISP). On an intranet system this is usually a log in page.
Search		Search – the greatest use of the Internet is to find things, to do this you will need to search; this gives you access to a search engine.

Microsoft Internet Explorer®	Firefox	Description
☆ Favorites	📖	Bookmarks/Favorites – this gives you access to the URLs stored by the browser.
🕐	🕐	History – this records every URL that the browser displays; it is useful if you find something and then need to go back to the source at a later time or date.
✉	Firefox does not have a specific email button.	Email – as email uses the same infrastructure as the Internet, it is possible to send or receive emails whilst browsing.
🖨	🖨	Print – it is sometimes useful and necessary to print a web page, but bear in mind that web pages are not all the same size, or A4, so always preview before printing.

Comparison of browser buttons

The very nature of HTML and the other web-based languages is that the pages themselves are 'dynamic'. A printed page from a book is 'flat': it can be read, but that is the limit to its functionality. A web page can look like a page from a book, but it can do so much more.

A web page can contain a variety of different media:

◆ text – typed text, formatted as it would be in a word-processed document;

◆ images – photographic quality pictures, manipulated to be appropriate for viewing on the screen;

◆ vector images – shapes and colours used to enhance the appearance of the page;

◆ animated video clips – using vector graphics;

◆ full-motion video;

◆ sounds;

◆ games;

◆ and just about anything else that can be transmitted electronically.

But even this is only like watching a television as opposed to reading a book – it's just as flat. What makes websites potentially more interesting is the ability to interact with what is going on using interactive components, such as forms, buttons and hyperlinks .

Any part of a web page can be turned into a hyperlink – often this is associated with text, but it can be anything – text, images, animation or a combination.

When a user moves their mouse pointer over the hyperlink the browser can detect it, and then carry out a function set within the code of the web page.

For example, moving the pointer over a small image can make it grow so that it can be seen more clearly. This type of 'rollover' is commonly used on buttons: as the pointer rolls over the button it may change its appearance, making it stand out from the rest of the page, therefore making it more likely that the user will press it.

This is a simple operation, a more complicated rollover is where a user moves the mouse pointer over a particular area of the screen and something happens in another part – this is called a 'disjointed rollover'.

Both of these show that the browser can capture movement. By clicking buttons on the screen you can also make the browser carry out a particular task, such as move you to another part of the web page or open another website.

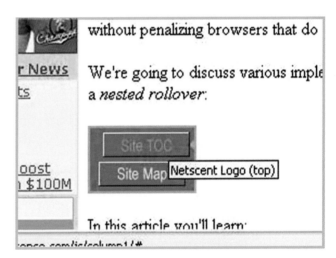

Rollover button

The design of a mouse allows users to point and click – exactly what a well-designed web page can take advantage of. The two operations give the user the ability to directly engage with the material on screen, enabling pages to become dynamic – the page can be different for every user.

Data capturing

The capability that a web page contains for capturing movement and action can be taken further through the use of forms.

A form can be built into a web page so that the user can complete it, the data is captured by the browser and it can be sent to the web server.

In this way web-based materials can become truly interactive: the response the user makes in the form can cause the web server to automatically search for a subsequent page and deliver it back to the user. This can make every user have a different experience on the same website.

This function also enables web pages to run searches.

Searching

Whether you choose to search using the toolbar on the browser or by going to a search page on a website, you are accessing the same functionality.

A search carried out by a web browser works in exactly the same way as a search on a database or spreadsheet.

The user enters the search criteria and the web browser sends the request to a web server. The web server then carries out the search, using specialist software on the server – a search engine .

As with searching a database, or running a query, the more detail you can add to the search criteria, the more likely it is that you will get a good result.

As mentioned earlier, asking for 'a book' will not be a very good request, so when searching for something specific, use specific criteria.

If you want to find the price of a new Ford car in Essex, a search should include a number of words, perhaps:

Ford new Essex

Capitalisation is irrelevant, but punctuation does make a difference. A full stop means 'and' so if you want the search for the three words, use full stops between Ford and new, and new and Essex.

If you request the search engine to look for a web page containing 'Ford and new and Essex', it will not return a page that has only 'Ford and Essex'.

There are other tricks to help organise your searching:

+ in front of a word means 'is required';

–- in front means 'is not required' (meaning it must not appear in the result);

" " quotation marks will restrict the search to finding exactly what appears inside the quotes;

* (asterisk) can be used as a 'wildcard', standing in for a word, when you are unsure of what should be in the search criteria.

There are a variety of different search engines, some of which specialise in particular areas of interest. The most popular general search engine at the moment is Google™ (www.google.co.uk), but also popular are Ask (www.ask.co.uk) and Ixquick (www.ixquick.com).

There are online telephone directories (www.192.com), business directories (www.scoot.co.uk) and all manner of others.

Tip

Try entering 'specialist search engines' as a search term into one of the search engines mentioned earlier.

Saving and printing

When you have found the page you were after, and it shows the information that your search requested, you will want to do something with it.

If you think you may need to come back to it at a later date, rather than using the 'history' function, you could save the URL in your bookmarks or favourites. This stores the URL and puts a hyperlink in your folder that you can click on to open the page.

You can also save the page 'for offline use'. If you do this a copy of the page is taken and stored in your temporary files, so that you can access it through your favourites/bookmarks in the same way, but it will not be updated if the actual page on the web server changes.

You may want just part of the page, in which case you could copy the particular section, as you would with any other document and paste it into a word-processed document. However, this will normally only copy the standard HTML of the page: anything like video or sound may be lost, as will much of the interactivity.

Copying and pasting is probably the most useful way to collect information from a site for use in your own work, as you can quickly gather small chunks of useful data. But you must remember to record where you got it from, so that you can acknowledge it in your own materials.

This is also a good method of building up a page for printing, as web pages are often odd sizes and printing the original page can be problematic.

Paste the web page screen grab into a document

If you must print the web page as it is, preview it first. If it seems that some of it is not going to print, it may be possible to do a screen grab (ALT and Print Screen), and then paste the screen grab into a document.

Homework

1 Make a web search to investigate the history of the Internet.

   a. Produce a milestone chart of the developments that have taken place to get the Internet to what it is today.

2 View the HTML behind the web page www.learn2.co.uk. See if you can work out when the site was built. Is any other information about the site to be found?

3 You should be aware of Internet security and personal safety issues. Check with your school or college for information and try a web search too.

4 Investigate the Edexcel site.

5 Use a search engine to gather a range of useful DiDA sites and record them in your favourites/bookmarks for future reference.

CHAPTER 15

Presentation software

What you will learn in this chapter

You will learn how to build a successful Microsoft PowerPoint® business presentation and how to avoid producing a poor slide show. The skill sections show you the basics of Microsoft PowerPoint® and how to relate the slide show to the target audience.

Introduction

Just about all businesses use presentation software, not only for presentations about products or services but also to help with training courses, or informing staff about changes and new initiatives. It is therefore a very useful tool for business. If used well, presentation software can make the difference between a show being understood and remembered by the audience or not. It can also be the difference between a business failing or succeeding.

In order for the presentation to do the job, the layout and planning of a presentation should be thorough. Layout and correct use of the many tools (many of which you have already used in Microsoft® Word) play a large part in presentations. The correct use of typography, colour, charts and images are of great importance. However, presentation software programs have all the tools a non-designer needs: pre-designed layouts, or templates as they are called, are already designed for specific types of presentation – you simply insert your text and/or images.

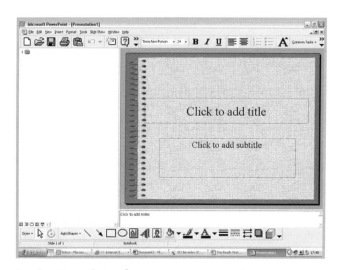

Design templates for a new presentation

However, having read this book, you should be able to lay out your own presentations from scratch without resorting to templates.

Using presentation software

Presentation software gives you control over the information you are displaying. It allows you to combine text, sound, graphics and moving images, and decide when and where they are to appear. However, your key points must always be presented in such a way that your audience will want to watch them and remember them.

Easier to read

Many people have poor eyesight and you must bear them in mind when creating a presentation. Even users with good eyesight may have problems seeing a presentation in certain conditions – rooms with no blinds, rooms with lights on and so on. So those who have some problems seeing text or images will need your help.

A little planning can solve these problems, and a thoughtful designer can enhance the visibility of materials to meet the audience's needs. Simple things like displaying text as a larger font size or using bold text can make reading easier. Graphics can be enlarged to fill the entire screen and lines can be made thicker.

Differences in colours and tones can also help. If there is little contrast between the subject and the background, viewing is more difficult. This is a common complaint of many people with poor vision, especially those in older age groups. Microsoft PowerPoint® lets you adjust contrast using black and white, shades of grey or a range of colour combinations. Displaying bright and bold colours for text or graphics against a light background can make the difference between readable and unreadable text for people with poor vision. This has already been mentioned in the chapters covering web design and in previous books, so if you want to refresh your memory take look at them.

Colour

Control of colour adds another important point to designing materials for a larger range of people. Children love brighter colours but some presentations may require a more sombre approach. Microsoft PowerPoint® provides a good way of getting around this problem. It lets a designer specify colours of the graphic parts. It is possible to make copies of the same graphics, or even of an entire presentation, and then change the colours to have different versions for different audiences.

Tip

Use space to emphasise a point.

Another way to increase the visibility of graphics is to avoid unreadable, busy or complex screens – a very common error! It is surprising how over-complicated some screens appear once people get the hang of using the software. It is easy to overdo it.

Animation

Microsoft PowerPoint® has a range of animation tools to create moving objects, similar to a cartoon, which bring life into presentations. Animation generally makes text and graphics more fun and can be used to focus the audience on certain points. Movement also helps to keep people's attention – especially useful given that most of us can only concentrate for up to 20 minutes anyway!

Graphics suitable for the audience

A business can fail simply by using a presentation that is inappropriate. Imagine trying to convince a group of investors that your products are great (which they may be) only to fail because the presentation did not get the point across!

Graphics can be developed from your own illustrations and photographs or obtained by purchasing them. Your source of images can be clip art, photographs and pictures that you scan in, photographs from a digital camera and so on.

Some software packages contain tens of thousands of clip-art images (Microsoft® Word has thousands free with its software). Even the best clip art can be unsuitable or not quite right, but you may be able to change it to suit. If it's vector based, you can change some parts, add bits from other clip-art pictures, and re-colour parts as desired. Re-colouring is especially useful for varying skin tones, for making graphics more age appropriate, and for making pictures easier to see.

Designing for small children

Children always enjoy looking at images. You can add surprise by designing fun into your presentation; add animation and keep it simple, make sure the words are easy to read, clear and use strong colours. Remember children may require long viewing times to absorb the information you are giving them. Children also may appreciate sound or music to make the points stick.

Involve your audience

Microsoft PowerPoint® lets you design materials in which your audience can play an active role and not just sit there staring at a screen! For example, if you can drag and drop onto a smart board, think about designing a slide containing many parts that are scattered around the screen. The challenge would be to drag the objects so they are paired correctly. An even more challenging approach is to design interactive buttons, each linked with a right or wrong answer. Clicking a button would result in the correct feedback: possibly a sound – clapping for a correct answer, and an appropriate sound for a wrong answer.

Tip

Keep slides uncluttered.

Tip

Presentation software such as Microsoft PowerPoint® is designed to present information to a specific audience. The design or feel of the presentation should always match the audience's needs. Projection is now commonplace and usually means that the slides are designed for screens larger than your PC monitor. However, this is not always the case as the presentation could be part of a web-based learning or marketing tool. You need to think carefully where your presentation will be viewed before designing.

Printouts

Remember to investigate the need for a printed version of the presentation – Microsoft PowerPoint® has a variety of different ways of producing hard copy – slides, handouts and note pages. Bear in mind that handouts containing multiple images of your slides will contain very small text – can your audience read it?

Templates

In Microsoft PowerPoint® you will find a huge range of tools that help you design unique presentations. Most of the tools are found across the range of Microsoft® software so starting to use Microsoft PowerPoint® is fairly easy. To make learning the software even easier there are ready-made backgrounds or formatted pages you can use that allow you to easily work at speed on a pre-designed theme. These are called templates. They have ready-made designs for specific themes. Your ideas are simply slotted into the designated areas on each page. However, as we have already mentioned, designing your own pages is often the key to success: you will be creating a unique piece of work capable of expressing your idea exactly.

Designing in Microsoft PowerPoint® is different to designing for paper pages. Pages in presentation software are always called slides; very appropriate these days as the projectors used are similar to the ones used to display photographic slides.

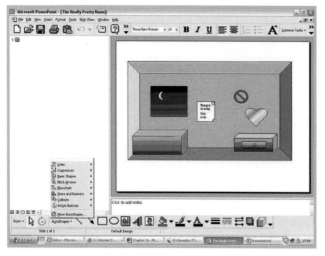

Title slide

Presentations on the web

Presentation software such as Microsoft PowerPoint® can also produce web pages; it is a very versatile tool. The way of doing this is the same as making a slide but it is saved as a web page and can be viewed in a browser to see what the page will look like on the web. You use the same tools and hyperlinks but present the slide as a web page. This lets your audience view the pages in a browser if they do not have Microsoft PowerPoint® software on their computers – not everyone has it.

Animation tools

Animation tools allow you to create movement with text objects or images. Sometimes, as we have already mentioned, people overdo these. Although fun, animation overkill can distract the audience from the points being made on your slide. You should use it as a point maker only or to reinforce information for the audience. The range of animation tools is quite large and adding these to images gives you a huge range of design options.

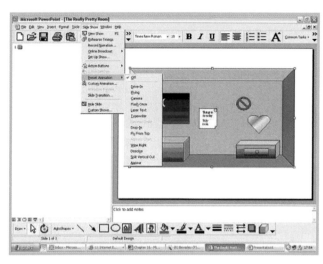

Animating objects in a presentation

Organising your presentation

One common way to organise your presentation is to start with general information and move towards specific information. Every slide should be limited to one major topic. Details can be presented as bullet points or numbered points. The slides must always explain your ideas with key words and phrases, not lots of text.

You should try to link the information you are presenting to information the audience already knows. If you are trying to explain something for the first time you will need to give lots of detail – something that Microsoft PowerPoint® is not very good at – so use simple phrases on the slides and explain the detail by talking to the audience.

It may also help to give out information on paper that can be referred to on the slides.

Remember Microsoft PowerPoint® can use:

✦ sounds

✦ images

✦ movies

✦ touch (if you use an interactive whiteboard)

✦ hyperlinked areas.

Tip

Try to keep to 36 words or less on each slide.

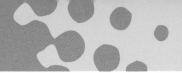

Top tips

Limit the use of serif fonts to headings or subheadings. Serifs are the little flicks on the top and bottom of text (Times, Times New Roman and Palatino). This is because screens are made up of dots and smaller parts of an image can become blurred. Try Helvetica, Arial and AvantGarde fonts.

CAPITAL LETTERS are harder to read easily. People generally read lower-case text better because it is similar to handwriting.

Avoid <u>underlined</u> text because it is used to indicate a hyperlink. Any clutter around a word will inevitably make it more difficult to read. To emphasise a point it is always better to use space!

Use bold, italics or colour to emphasise text.

Keep your font size as large as possible. The recommended smallest type size is 24 point.

Get someone to check your presentation from the back of the room to make sure it is clearly visible and report back any other problems.

Keep the slides as simple as possible.

Design a house style. Create a simple colour scheme with three or four colours. Establish a regular colour for titles, subtitles and text. If too many colours are used, the viewer will be unsure of the main focus.

Select a background or theme that relates to your presentation.

Make sure any template you use is appropriate to the content so that it does not confuse the audience. The text and selected images should be the focus of your presentation.

Light text on a dark background is easier for the viewer to read, but may require a darkened room. Do not mix slides with dark and light backgrounds because the sudden bright light will strain viewers' eyes.

Practising your presentation

Things can and do go wrong! Always practise with the equipment; practice will increase your confidence, giving you time to focus on the slides not the technology. Have a backup plan for equipment failures or electrical faults; what would you do if you had a group of people from around the world waiting for your presentation and the projector bulb blew? Hopefully you would have notes and handouts of the slides so you could carry on.

Remember visual effects and sound tracks; QuickTime® videos are large files that could increase the chances of something going wrong.

Do you want to encourage audience participation? Some presenters only average three minutes per slide and others cover three slides per minute. If you do want your audience to talk to you or ask questions, you should allow more time for the viewing. There are no rules for timing – you will have to apply common sense. Audiences process information at different rates: children may be quicker or slower to understand the content; older people may have large variations in absorbing information; people from different countries to whom your language is their second will take longer to absorb information. Bear these points in mind.

Tip

Always allow your audience time to read the slide, listen to your talk and take notes.

Evaluating your presentation

Probably the most important rule! Before presenting your work, get a friend or colleague to help you evaluate what you have done. After reviewing your presentation, ask yourself, can I make it any better? Think about revisions that can help you achieve your objectives more effectively. Are the important points emphasised well? Are the order and content presented sensibly? Have you got an introduction and conclusion? Would it benefit the audience to have a handout of the slides before the show?

Lost presentations

How can we find a lost presentation? It happens to us all: we forget a file or where we put it – bad news for DiDA candidates. But you can find your lost files by looking for a preview in the Open dialogue box.

Go to File and Open – the dialogue box will list the files in a particular folder. If you can remember the folder, navigate to it in the Look in: dropdown box. By clicking on the Views button the different data associated with the files will be displayed – one of the Views options is to show a Preview of the first slide. This can be very helpful in finding that lost presentation! The other way is to use the Search facility available from the Start menu – this can search the whole network for a missing file. Remember that it's best to not to lose it in the first place! Always give your files an appropriate filename and save them in a suitable folder.

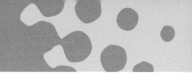

Homework

1   Select a template and try to follow the wizard's instructions to make a simple presentation. You can choose the subject. Then try doing the same with a blank sheet as a starting point but creating your own design.

2   Design a slide using a serif typeface then copy it and change the font to a sans serif typeface. See if it makes any difference.

3   Put two simple messages on a slide and try to make them as powerful a graphic image as you can. Use text, colour and images.

CHAPTER 16

Project planning

What you will learn in this chapter

This chapter will explore some of the uses of software designed to help you manage your work. As mentioned in earlier chapters, planning your work is essential. If you do not have a clear idea of where you are going, you will not know when you have arrived!

Planning ahead

How structured a plan is can vary widely, but it can be helpful to think of it in terms of going shopping. Making a list before you set out can be a great advantage, as it keeps you focused. If you have time to wander around a shop, without a list, it might be very enjoyable, but it is easy to forget some of the things you wanted to buy. Planning a project is a bit like this: if you want to stay focused and achieve what you set out to do – develop a tightly structured plan.

To help you develop a plan there is a range of software applications that you can use to manage your workload.

Workflow

The way that a project moves from start to finish is sometimes described as the 'workflow'. Another comparison might be useful here. Imagine a river: at the beginning it is a small stream, bubbling and full of life; then it widens and the water gets deeper, and the volume of water increases, but the water seems to move more slowly. The river becomes broad and powerful, and finally runs into the sea, but the fresh water quickly mixes with the salt water from the sea, and the river no longer exists.

A project is very similar: the start is exciting, creative and full of possibilities. The middle of the project is where the real work happens, and it can seem dull and uninspiring. The end is marked by the completion of the project – the solution to the original problem becomes mainstream and it is difficult to think of a time when the solution was not in place.

Along the way there are times when IT can help you to guide the workflow.

Mind-mapping software

At the beginning it can be difficult to focus your thoughts and find direction. At this point, mind-mapping software can be very helpful. Mind-mapping software is designed to record lots of interlinked material. In its simplest form it is a web of words, each linked to a central theme or context.

MindManager

The software helps you to develop a system of visualising your knowledge and the links between different aspects of a single concept. It can use words or images, along with colours and other graphical elements to express your ideas. This can be an effective way of communicating a summary of information, at a stage in the project when it may be difficult to convey the meaning in any other form.

The software can be used to manage projects, run meetings and organise apparently random thoughts or lists into coherent patterns. It can even be used to develop a website. One of the most common mind-mapping applications is MindManager.

How to develop a mind map

You may have used 'brainstorms' or 'mind showers' in other subjects, particularly design and technology – these are usually done as a group activity, with the teacher recording the results on the board, for all to see. A mind map is a similar sort of thing.

You begin with the central theme that you wish to investigate. For example, if your project is an enterprise activity based on selling toys on a website, you could build two separate mind maps to help you – one with 'toys' as the central theme, another focusing on 'websites'. From the central theme you then add spurs – offshoots that carry the main ideas which are related to the central theme.

For the 'toys' map you could add the following:

✦ children

✦ colours

✦ boys/girls

✦ price

✦ packaging

✦ dolls

✦ models

✦ board games

✦ TV link.

From the spurs you can then add further details to clarify your ideas – these are called 'branches'. The toys map has a spur labelled 'children'; from here you could add branches for the following:

✦ ages

✦ tastes

✦ favourite TV programmes

✦ safety.

The more information you can include at this point, the more useful your mind map will be.

Using mind-mapping software

At its simplest level, mind-mapping software is a way of recording your thoughts, for your own use. In previous chapters and in other books in this series we have mentioned keeping a scrapbook or sketchbook, and storing collections of images electronically – using mind-mapping software, you can use all these collected thoughts to illustrate your ideas. The power of the software enables you to add images, colours and different effects to the diagram, in order to make it more representative of what you are trying to record.

The software can also be used to integrate your mind map with other applications. For example, MindManager provides the facility to merge your mind map with

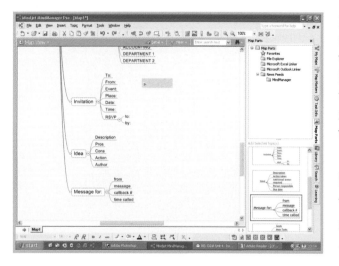

MindManager (2)

Microsoft® Project, a professional project management application. This means that when you have put as much detail as possible into your mind map, you can choose to export the data into Microsoft® Project, and synchronise existing Microsoft® Project files with your mind map.

Generating web pages

You can also use MindManager to export your mind map as a web page, as set out below:

1 Develop your mind map; include images, colours and as much detail as you can.

2 Save the file and make sure that you have a destination folder for the web page. (The application will generate a number of files and it is important that they are kept together.)

3 Go to File, Export and choose Web page.

4 Change the Save in: folder to the one that you have already set up, then run the export.

5 When the application has generated the required files and made the links, it will open a browser window and you will be able to see your new website.

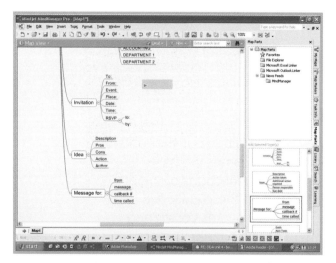

Example of a mind-map-generated website

The MindManager application will generate a number of files in order to make the website. The number will vary depending on how much information you have included in your mind map. Some of these files can be edited in your web design application, such as Macromedia Dreamweaver®, or even in Notepad, if you know how to work with raw HTML.

Planning and milestones

One of the more interesting aspects of the MindManager application is that all the help files and tutorials are built from mind maps themselves. It is worth having a look through them, just to see what can be done – there is even one on project management!

Once you have developed your project mind map, you should have enough information to start to put together a proper project plan (see Chapter 9). It is important to keep in mind that you can change your plan, and developing a new mind map at each stage may be a good way to refocus your thoughts. For example, you could generate a mind map for each milestone – the points when you check how your plan is unfolding and if you will meet your deadlines. You might decide to create two mind maps for each milestone – one to show what you have achieved so far, and one to show what will be happening next. These can be included in your e-portfolio as evidence.

Organising your e-portfolio

The website generator explored above could be used to organise your e-portfolio, as follows:

✦ Generate a mind map for the e-portfolio.

✦ Export the mind map as a web page.

✦ Edit the website using Macromedia Dreamweaver®.

✦ Add detail to the pages as you progress through the project, harvesting new evidence.

The website generator creates a home page and then a navigation panel. The navigation panel is developed from each of the spurs or, if there are any, from each branch. The content of the branch becomes the content of the web page that is reached via the link in the navigation panel.

This selection of files can be amended easily, so it can reflect more detail than the original mind map. (The whole idea of a mind map is to note down your thoughts quickly, so the original mind map can be generated in minutes.) In a short space of time, you will have a simple, clearly defined website, with a page for each of the ideas you listed in the mind map. As the project unfolds you can refine the site, adding or removing pages and content, until you have a fully functioning e-portfolio.

Mind-map files

Testing

It would be a good idea to include a branch on the mind map for testing or checking. This will become an important part of the resulting website, as you can use the page to record any tests that you carry out along the way, as you develop your business or enterprise activity. It can also be used to record changes that you make to the plan. Remember that any change must be justified, and the easiest way to do this is to carry out a test and find that something does not meet the requirements.

For example, if you are developing a set of documents for an organisation and part-way through the project you find that the colours you have chosen do not look right, you will need to change the design and perhaps take the new ideas back to the client. This might be recorded in one of the following ways:

1 I changed the colour scheme and asked the client if they liked it.

2 I tested the colour scheme with a potential customer and the results showed that the customer did not like the combination; I then redesigned the leaflet and have resubmitted it to the client for checking.

Which way do you think demonstrates a better standard of working?

Timelines and Gantt charts

Testing or checking the different elements of your plan as you work may have an impact on your schedule, so you need to make sure that any changes you make to your plan are recorded on your timeline. This will make it easier for you to predict 'crunch' points, and it also shows the moderator that you have made a plan, and then amended it, but that you have kept to the deadlines throughout.

Timelines can be very simple systems, but they can also be very powerful. In industry a formalised timeline system is often used – this is known as the Gantt chart.

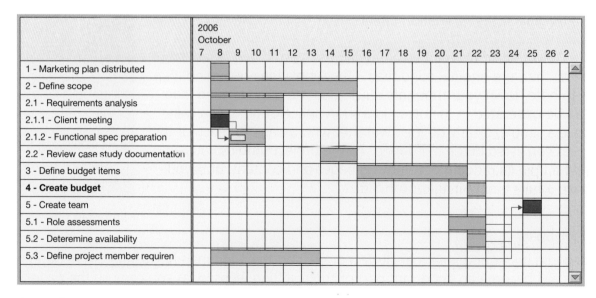

Gantt chart

The Gantt chart is named after the developer, Henry L. Gantt, who first used one to illustrate a production activity around 1910. His charts were relatively simple – not much more than linked timelines. With modern computer power and applications, the Gantt chart can now be used as a very powerful way of estimating progress.

A timeline is a single line, with a start point and an end point, with some milestones marked along the way. A Gantt chart is a series of lines representing activities, arranged with the earliest at the top and those planned later at the bottom. This arrangement allows for more realistic planning, as a project often has different types of activity, some of which are interrelated and some of which stand alone.

When making a cup of tea, for example, there are many different activities involved; four of these are listed below:

✦ Boil the water.

✦ Place the tea bag in a cup.

✦ Add sugar.

✦ Add milk.

A timeline can only show the starting and finishing points of one activity at a time, otherwise it becomes confusing.

A Gantt chart can be used to show the same activities, but in a clearer format.

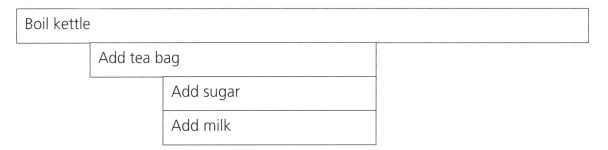

This simple Gantt chart shows that a number of activities can take place at the same time, whereas the timeline appears to show that each individual activity must be completed before the next one begins – something that could create confusion.

When it is important to finish one activity before starting another, however, Gantt charts make this easy to see. This is shown by adding relationships between activities.

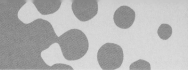

For example, another relatively simple operation is making toast:

✦ Cut bread.

✦ Toast bread.

✦ Butter bread.

Here, each stage is entirely dependent on the previous stage being completed, as shown in the Gantt chart below.

It may seem obvious, but it would be silly to butter the bread before it had finished being toasted!

Although you may have access to some advanced software for project management, such as Microsoft® Project, a Gantt chart can be designed and maintained using Microsoft® Word or Microsoft Excel®.

There are some simple rules to follow when using Gantt charts:

✦ The total time for the project – the terminal element – is the top line of the chart, showing the beginning and the end of the project. This is usually measured in weeks.

✦ The summary elements – each task or activity that takes place through the life of the project – are listed below the terminal element, in the order in which they are to be carried out. However, there can be exceptions to this rule: if a series of tasks are related, but grouping them together would cause them to be out of sequence, you will need to decide which method of recording the tasks would be the clearest.

✦ Where a task's start point is dependent on the completion of another task, this should be shown with an arrow.

A Gantt chart can be adapted easily to become an **interactive** element in a web page. Each task can be hyperlinked to a page with greater detail. This would be a great way of illustrating what you have planned to do – and as the project progresses you can add alterations at each stage. The resulting web pages would be full of good evidence of planning, evaluating and testing – all necessary elements for your assessment.

Homework

1 Produce a mind map of your favourite hobby or pastime.

2 Produce a timeline for your school day – mark on the timeline important points, such as lesson changeovers.

3 Produce a Gantt chart for making your breakfast or another meal.

Spreadsheet software

What you will learn in this chapter

In this chapter you will learn how to use Microsoft Excel® for the production of charts and to work with data. The chapter also looks at other ways you can use Microsoft Excel® creatively.

What is a spreadsheet?

Accountants have used large lined sheets of paper called spreadsheets for hundreds of years. They used to write with ink and calculated in their heads or with beads. They were skilled individuals and took an enormous amount of time doing their sums!

A Microsoft Excel® spreadsheet

Computerised or electronic spreadsheets started in the 1970s and were clumsy and slow. In accounting jargon a spreadsheet was a large sheet of paper with columns and rows that organised information about transactions for business people to work from. A spreadsheet can show all of the costs of a transaction on a single sheet of paper in a clear and organised way for a manager to examine when making a decision.

Business relies heavily on spreadsheets and it could be argued that spreadsheets along with databases are almost irreplaceable in today's business world.

A spreadsheet is just as likely to be used for creating graphics for presentations to show the data recorded as charts with annotations. They are widely used in conjunction with presentation packages such as Microsoft PowerPoint®. Spreadsheets are very powerful tools and can also be used to do calculations or have programs written within the spreadsheets called macros. So for DiDA you will probably use a spreadsheet for creating graphs from data you have collected perhaps from a survey or questionnaire. You may also use them for creating lists or calculating information obtained during your research. Spreadsheet graphics can be pasted into most other software, for example Microsoft PowerPoint®, Microsoft® Word, web software and so on. As the basics of spreadsheets work the same as most other software, cutting, copying and pasting use the same processes as you would in any other piece of software:

◆ Cut = CTRL+X

◆ Paste = CTRL+V

◆ Copy = CTRL+C

Electronic spreadsheets such as Microsoft Excel® organise information into software-defined columns and rows: columns go up and down, rows go across.

Information can be added up across or up and down by a formula to give a total or sum (a bit like using a calculator). The spreadsheet program can sum up information from many paper sources in one place and present the information in a format to help you see the whole picture for the project you may be working on.

Microsoft Excel® can be used for:

◆ graphics (charts)

◆ linking to web pages (hyperlinks)

◆ adding up

◆ multiplying

◆ dividing

◆ subtracting.

Working with spreadsheet graphics

The graphics possibilities that Microsoft Excel® offers you are probably going to be well used in your DiDA course. They are easy to use and look very good. The making of graphs from data is very straightforward and, providing you choose an easy-to-understand graph, will help make your data clearer.

Excel has drawing tools identical to those found in Microsoft® Word which can be used to highlight cells or add interest to certain points. However you are more likely to insert clip art or create charts. You can insert several kinds of graphics into a Microsoft Excel® document: graphics files that you have already saved, clip art that comes with Microsoft® Office, or AutoShapes from the drawing toolbox.

Microsoft Excel® Drawing toolbar

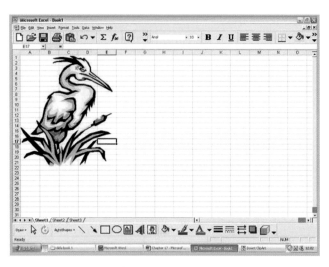

Graphic in a spreadsheet

Inserting a graphics file

To insert a graphic into a spreadsheet:

Select where the graphics is to go and click on that area.

Choose Insert > Picture > From File.

Find the file then select it.

Click Insert.

Tip

To more easily move a graphics file, insert a text box first. With the text box selected, insert the file.

To insert clip art:

Select Insert > Picture > Clip Art.

Select a category, and then choose a picture.

Click Insert.

To insert an AutoShape:

Click the Drawing button on the Standard toolbar to display the Draw toolbar.

Click AutoShapes then the category and shape you want to insert.

To change a graphics file or clip art:

Select it.

You can then resize it using the handles.

You can use the Picture toolbar (same as in Microsoft® Word) to modify the image in many ways, including cropping, brightening, contrast and so on.

To remove a graphic:

Select it.

Press DELETE.

To rotate a graphic:

Select it.

Select Rotate or Flip from the Draw tab.

Select Free Rotate .

Drag the green circles to the rotation you want.

Formatting

Formatting has to do with setting text or background fonts and colours. As we all seem to have colour screens and colour printers we can have huge array of resources availed to us. The problem with this is the same as the problems we mentioned with presentation software: people get carried away with too many colours and too many fonts that become illegible.

You can use colour in Microsoft Excel® to highlight columns by selecting the column on the top grey bar with a letter on it and dipping into the colour palette. Selecting the grey letter boxes is a bit like highlighting text in word-processing documents: it informs the computer you wish to apply formatting to that selected area.

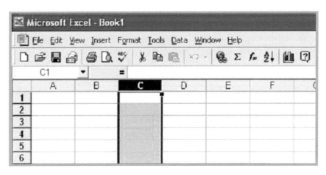

Select a column

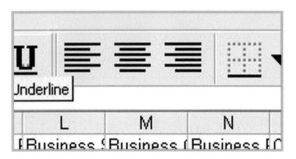

Aligning cell contents

Aligning

To align the contents of the cells (make them centred, range to the right or left, or fully justify them) is the same process as in word possessing. Click on the icons on the Formatting toolbar.

Adding borders

Adding a border can give a focus to your work in the worksheet. To add a border, highlight your work by dragging the mouse diagonally from the top right to bottom left of your work, then go to the Formatting toolbar and find the Borders icon and drop-down menu. There is a range of options to choose from. To add a colour, click Fill Colour on the formatting toolbar while your work is still highlighted.

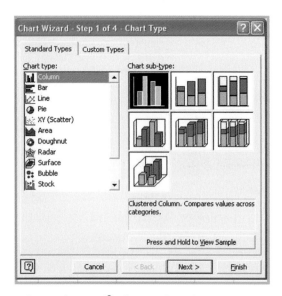

Microsoft Excel® Chart Wizard

Merging

You may wish to make one or more cells into one – this is called merging. To merge cells simply highlight the cells you wish to merge and click on Merge and Centre on the Formatting toolbar. This is always useful for creating title bars at the top of your worksheet.

Making a chart

Once you have created a simple list of text and number values – perhaps the result of a DiDA survey – you may want to create a chart. We tend to call charts 'graphs' but because Microsoft Excel® is used throughout the world, the term 'chart' is used. The simple way to create a chart is to highlight your work then click on the Chart Wizard on either the Standard or Formatting toolbar.

The Chart Wizard gives you a range of different charts to choose from. It is very important that you choose the right chart for your presentation or publication, so some thought should go into deciding which type is most appropriate – an unnecessarily complex chart can be confusing. As you go through the Chart Wizard you will be offered a range of text and graphics options. Choose these if you wish or keep clicking on Next then Finish. Your chart will be in colour. Once you have your chart you can copy or cut and paste it into any publication, presentation package or web page.

The main rules for showing data graphically are:

✦ always keep the charts simple;

✦ do not use scripts or difficult-to-read text;

✦ think about the age of your audience or market;

✦ never give too much information at a time;

✦ try to incorporate the graphics from the Drawing toolbar to help make things clearer.

Splitting and freezing panes

Sometimes your worksheet can become too big to see and will not fit onto one screen. This problem is solved by splitting the worksheet into smaller, scrollable sections. To do this go to Window and click on Split and the worksheet will be divided up into four panes instead of the normal one, rather like having four mini spreadsheets.

Splitting panes may be useful when you are working on several pieces of work at the same time. The panes are all scrollable.

To see two hidden parts of a large worksheet at once, you can split the screen and scroll separately in each pane. You can split the screen vertically or horizontally. This is really useful when you have large amounts of information and saves time.

To split the screen into two panes, drag the split box at the top of the vertical scrollbar or the right of the horizontal scrollbar to the position you need it. Look at the cursor; you will see it changes to a split arrow as you drag.

Formatting a page

If you wish to format a page, select File > Page Set-up. You can then select from a range of

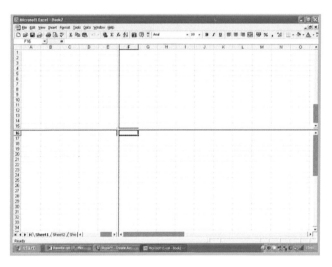

Splitting panes

Tip

You can lock row and column headings so you can view them no matter how far down or to the right you scroll.

If you want to freeze column headings only, click the cell in the first column just below the headings.

To freeze column and row headings, just click the cell just below and to the right of the headings.

Select Window > Freeze Panes.

If you would like to unfreeze the headings, select Window > Unfreeze Panes.

formatting options including Orientation , Scaling , Margins and Headers/Footers , and printing options including Print titles , Gridlines , Row and column headings and Page order . Click on OK when you're finished.

Microsoft Excel® viewer

The Microsoft Excel® Viewer allows you to open, view, and print Microsoft Excel® spreadsheets, even if you or the person you are sending a worksheet to does not have Microsoft Excel® installed. You can copy data from the Viewer to another program. But you cannot edit data, save a workbook or create a new workbook. This download is on Microsoft®'s main site and is free.

Formulas

In Microsoft Excel® all formulas start with the equals sign (=). This tells Excel that you wish to enter a formula in the cell and not a value.

To do a simple sum you will always need to put in one of these mathematical signs:

/ (slash) for divisions
* (asterisk) for multiplication
+ (plus sign) for addition
– (minus sign) for subtraction
% for percentages.

This is much the same as you would use in a paper calculation except for the slash symbol, which is always used for division.

Tip

With formulas you must always state the column first then the row.

Do not include spaces in a formula, as these will mess the calculations up.

Excel formulas always use relative referencing by default. Relative references always update themselves if moved.

Absolute references never update even if moved. Absolute references reference the same cell address, no matter where the formula is in the spreadsheet.

Absolute references are always shown as a dollar ($) sign preceding the row and/or column designation.

AutoSum function

Excel has a shortcut to make it easy to add rows or columns of figures together – the AutoSum function.

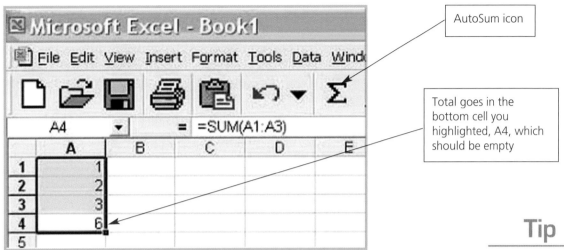

Using AutoSum to add up a column of figures

Select the numbers you want to add up and the cell for the answer. Click on the AutoSum icon (a sigma sign, looking like an M standing on its side) and the answer will appear in the bottom cell (if you are summing a column) or right-hand cell (if you are summing a row).

Printing your worksheets

To check what your sheet will look when printed, always first click on print preview.

To print out your worksheet and not the whole worksheet available (which may print out pages of blank or lined sheets), highlight the work you wish to print and choose File > Print Area .

Printed page set-up

You can also set pages to landscape or portrait or scale margins and so on. In this area you can also select the option of printing the guidelines seen on the normal worksheet or removing them.

To change the worksheet's name, first double-click the worksheet's tab and type a new name.

Tip

The bit many beginners get wrong is that they do not leave an empty cell for the answer to go in, so always include a cell directly below the numbers you want to add up (or to the right of a row of numbers). This makes it the active cell.

Using worksheets and workbooks

To move quickly through the worksheets, click the tabs at the bottom.

To insert (add) a worksheet within a workbook, choose Insert > Worksheet .

Use Microsoft Excel® creatively

To select a worksheet, click its tab. To select several worksheets at a time, click the first worksheet's tab, press and hold down Shift and click the last worksheet's tab.

If you need to you could design posters, or write letters and booklets in Microsoft Excel®. That is not what it was designed to do but as it has many of the same tools as Microsoft® Word, Microsoft PowerPoint® and Microsoft® Publisher this is possible but not recommended!. Microsoft Excel® can be used for producing lists of information and it is easy to insert images including photos and clips or scanned images, so try to use it creatively. You do not have to use it purely for number crunching.

Homework

1 List a group of favourite sweets (minimum of 12) and sort them alphabetically. Format the list using fonts, alignment and colour in the row.

2 Open up a column and row and add colours or shades, borders and a clip-art image to make a simple poster.

3 Produce a simple chart from data on family or friends' birth dates and months – minimum of 15 people. Sort into highest to lowest month for birthdays and produce a chart. Place the chart into Microsoft PowerPoint®.

Tip

If you grab the right-hand bottom corner of a cell once you have written January, Microsoft Excel® will automatically put in the other months of the year for you as you drag down.

CHAPTER 18

Website software

What you will learn in this chapter

This chapter is concerned with developing an online presence, using appropriate software to produce websites. You will learn about web-design software and what software does which job best. You will come across words or jargon, which will be explained, and you will get tips on designing web pages.

Introduction

In designing and making a product, you will need to balance many conflicting aspects. You will also need to consider a whole range of rules.

Before you can even start to design a web page you need to have content. What will your page have on it? You don't need to be precise at this point, but you need some idea.

Earlier chapters have mentioned the need for gathering resources; web design is an area where you need to start early. You may need to collect text from one source and images from somewhere else, video and sounds from other places. You may also need to generate your own movies and audio tracks.

Other chapters of this book explain the structure you could consider for storing your material. When using web software, you will need to be very organised, as the links that are generated between pages will only work if the web structure stays rock solid.

Load time

The most important thing to bear in mind when developing web-based multimedia products is, 'How long will it take for the page to load?' If what you produce takes so long to load that the user clicks off it, it doesn't matter what else you have done, because nobody will ever see it!

This aspect of site design is called 'optimising'. It is the operation of making sure that everything on your page works well together and loads quickly.

Most Internet users will only wait a few seconds for a page to load on their screen. The average wait time is 8 seconds; this means that if your web page takes more than 8 seconds to load, the average user will start to click their mouse and move to another page. One way around this is to have things loading quickly to keep their attention, even though the whole page takes a little longer. Reading this paragraph will have taken more than 8 seconds!

There are a number of websites that offer to check your load times; most professional sites use some sort of optimisation software, and are therefore able to keep their load times very short. Two of the most popular sites in the UK are shown below:

www.google.co.uk takes less than 3 seconds to load.
www.bbc.co.uk takes less than 5 seconds to load.

This time constraint is difficult to plan for, but should be considered at every stage in designing a web page or website. The designer should always have at the back of their mind, 'How long will this take?'

Google™ and BBC websites

Designing a page

Web pages are very simple to make. They can be generated using a word-processor application or graphics program, and then saved in an appropriate format for viewing through a browser.

There are a number of professional web-design applications that you will be using if you want to specialise in this area – Adobe Dreamweaver® (used to be Macromedia Dreamweaver®) or Adobe GoLive®, for example.

Many web designers consider layout to be the most important aspect of design after load time. When you use a web-design application the first thing you are asked is what layout you will be working with.

Whatever you design it must be clear and easy to understand. If you look around on the Internet you will soon find pages that you can understand and others that are confusing and poorly layed out.

The way most Western people see the world is the way they read – top to bottom, left to right. This also applies to websites; the most important information should be at the top, the left should be for secondary information and the bottom right for the general material.

If you look at newspapers, magazines and web pages there is a common feel to the way they look.

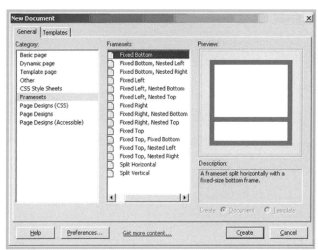

Selecting a layout in Dreamweaver®

A common feel to the way they look

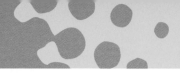

A common feel to the way they look

When a web page is built the designer usually takes cues from things around them:

✦ If you want to design a page that carries lots of text, like a newspaper, then you should look at newspapers and similar publications to get a feel for the ways that they communicate their information.

✦ If your page is mostly images, then look at catalogues and magazines to see how they work.

✦ If you are developing pages that have video or sound – watch the television. Many programmes have particular 'page layouts' – Sky News or BBC News 24 have running headlines across the bottom of the page. Credit pages generally run right to left or bottom to top.

Pages that carry a mixture of text and images are the most difficult to design well. Again, for inspiration look through magazines and other publications.

Designing your layout should be done on paper; most designers are pretty good at art – the creative eye. But it is not essential; being able to sketch your ideas really helps.

When you start to transfer the idea onto the computer, there are lots of helpful guides and templates that you can use.

When you have some idea of layout, you need to get working on the content.

Content

The way the site files are stored and operate can have an influence over the speed that your pages load.

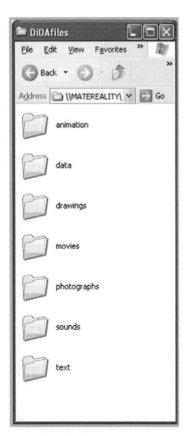

Website folders

Within your main folder you need at least two subdirectories:

✦ Images – where you will keep all the pictures that will be used on your site.

✦ Pages – where all the individual pages will be stored.

But, as you are probably going to want to involve a number of other elements, you should consider using more folders.

In the first book in this series, *Using ICT,* a simple, static website was developed using Adobe Dreamweaver®.

Below are some ideas for how to add some multimedia elements.

When developing a multimedia product you should start by working out exactly what is needed to construct each page. This is best done using a 'storyboard'.

A storyboard is a document, usually handwritten or drawn, that shows what will be on each page.

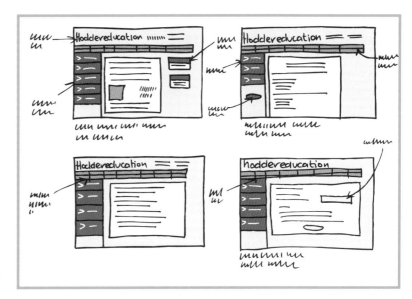

Website storyboard

Building a website using Adobe Dreamweaver®

Home page

Adobe Dreamweaver® can be set up in a number of different ways; we have used the default design view.

When working with Adobe Dreamweaver®, or any other web-design application, the software is set up to build a multipage site. You have already set up a simple folder structure, and will now be using that as you build your page. The same structure will allow you to build a fully functioning multipage site.

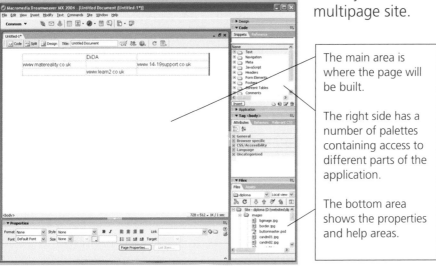

The main area is where the page will be built.

The right side has a number of palettes containing access to different parts of the application.

The bottom area shows the properties and help areas.

Adobe Dreamweaver® desktop

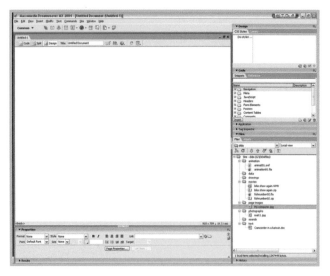

Creating a web page

Click on File , New – a dialogue box will appear offering a variety of options. Choose Basic Page and Create .

The blank page will appear as a white background, the top of which holds the page title – as it has not been saved yet, it is 'untitled-1'.

Save the blank page in your root folder, not your pages folder. The index page should be kept separate from the other pages, so that it can be easily accessed for updating. Save your page as Index.htm – the new title should appear on the tab.

You may also notice that the title of the page remains 'untitled document'; this is the title that will be shown by a search engine so to be a little more professional, it is good practice to change that. It does not have to match the filename, so call it 'DiDA resource'.

The Properties inspector below the page changes as you work, so to make sure that we start off with the correct properties section, move your mouse pointer to the middle of the page and right click. From the shortcut menu choose Page Properties .

This dialogue allows you to set various properties for the page; later we will set properties for elements that will be appearing on the page.

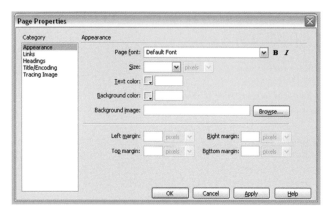

Page Properties dialogue box

Firstly, set the appearance of the page.

Choose a font – we are going to produce a DiDA resource, so we need a professional-looking font. Arial is a good bet – it looks good and is available on most computers.

The size is not important at this point, but colour is. Blue can be much easier to work with, and can also help people who have difficulty reading.

Click on the colour picker next to Text color and choose a font colour.

Do the same with Background color; a pale yellow goes well with the blue text.

The rest can stay as they are.

Click Apply and the background should change to the colour you picked.

The other settings can be dealt with later, so click OK .

Typing straight onto the background is the easiest way to build your page, but it can create difficulties later. So it is much better to enter text into a table. A table can be formatted or moved easily.

On the toolbar click the Table button; another dialogue box will appear.

This table will contain the title and a short message, so choose two rows and one column.

Rather than having the text run right onto the edge of the page, if you make the table less than 100 per cent you can have a proportion of space down the sides, so choose 85 per cent.

The table should be invisible, so leave the other settings as 0.

Adobe Dreamweaver® has a number of helpful additions to enable designers to make their pages accessible to all users. In the Summary box add, 'This is the homepage for our DiDA resource'. Click OK .

Your table will appear as a dotted boundary at the top of your page. The insertion point will be flashing in the top left cell, aligned left.

Click on the border of the cells and the table will be highlighted. The Properties inspector will have altered to show settings for the table, rather than the contents of the table.

To make the table appear centrally at the top of the page click Centre in the Align box.

It is also a good idea to give your table identification; in the Table Id box enter 'title block'.

You can now start to enter text directly into the table.

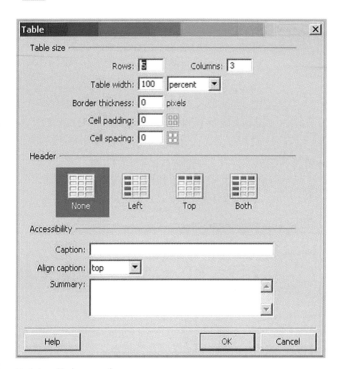

Table dialogue box

Table in web page

Start with a title in the top cell. Then enter some text into the second cell.

The Properties inspector allows you to format the text as in a word processor, so try out the different options until you have your text looking how you would like it.

When you are happy, press F12 to preview your page in a browser. You may have to save the page before it can be previewed.

If you resize the browser window, you will see that the text automatically reflows – this is one of the reasons for using a table to place the text. If the text goes straight onto the background it will not reflow so easily.

By centring the table you can see that the title remains central, even if the page is resized.

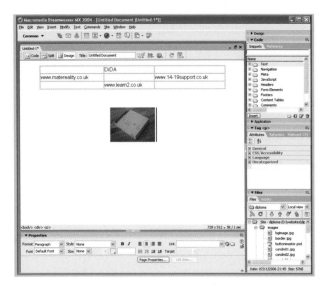

Below the table we need to add an image.

Click on the Image icon on the toolbar and a dialogue will open up, displaying your folders.

Navigate to your images folder and select an image. Click OK.

If your images are straight from a digital camera, or scanned, they may be far too large for a web page. If they are, or even if they just need a bit of tweaking, Adobe Dreamweaver® has the ability to jump straight into Adobe Fireworks® to edit the image.

The image that has been brought in here is far too large. The Properties inspector has a button to Edit in Fireworks . Click on it. If you do not have this application, you will need to edit it in another graphics package.

Tip

Resizing the image in Adobe Dreamweaver® will not reduce the file size, so although the image may be visually smaller, the actual file may still be many megabytes.

Adobe Fireworks® will open and display your image. You can now edit the image to make it more suitable for use.

The image straight from a digital camera can be very large, but for use on this page it needs to be approximately 5 cm wide, at 72 dots per inch (DPI). After adjusting in Adobe Fireworks®, it is automatically updated in Adobe Dreamweaver®.

Remember load speed is important, so images need to be small and of a low resolution; 72 DPI is perfect for on-screen images.

When you are happy with the size of the image, you can think about positioning it where you want it.

When it is in place, click on it and go to the Properties inspector and click in the Alt box. Enter a title or explanation for the image that can be read by a screen reader for users that do not show images in their browser, or for visually impaired users.

As in word-processing packages, an image is seen as a character. It is moved in the same way as a typed letter is moved. Again it may be best to place it in a table, as this will allow it to be moved more easily.

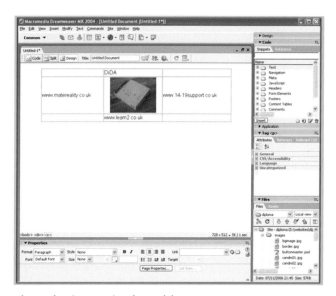

Place the image in the table

To add rows to your existing table, click in the bottom cell and press TAB – as in most other applications, a new row is added.

Now it's time to add more information – not much as this is the home page. We just need to add something about what can be found on the other pages we will be developing at a later date.

As you can see, more text has been added, and the format of the text has been altered to make it look more appropriate.

The list of DiDA units has been made into a bulleted list. This makes it clear that each title is separate, but they are all part of the same qualification.

Adding more information

The sentence about the following pages has been made bold to catch the reader's eye; it is important that the reader sees that there are other pages to look at.

The page links have been entered into their own cell. This involved splitting the cell, using the button on the Properties inspector and making four cells in the bottom row.

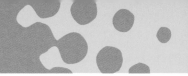

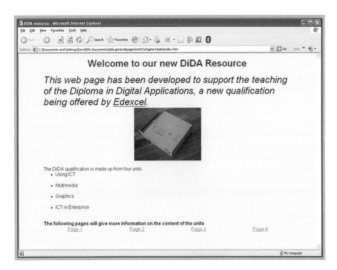

Viewing the page in a web browser

When you have added some detail to your page, press F12 to view it as it would be seen over the Internet.

As it now appears there will be at least four more pages to this site we had better build them!

Before starting work on a new page, make sure you have saved your home page.

Other pages

The remaining pages of this website are only going to contain a little content; they can be added to at a later date. They are purely to illustrate how linking works.

Page 1

In Adobe Dreamweaver® go to File , New (or CTRL+N), Basic Page , Create .

Save the new page in your 'pages' folder, as 'page 1'.

Change the Title to 'Page 1 of the DiDA Resource'.

Add a table with two rows and four columns.

Merge the middle two cells of the top row.

Add an image from your images folder; you may need to edit the image as with the image on the home page. Remember to add a comment in the Alt box of the Properties inspector.

In the four cells on the second row add the text:

Home

Page 2

Page 3

Page 4

As this is page 1, it doesn't need a link to page 1, but it does need a link back to the home page.

Format the page and table to make it all look better than the default settings.

Pages 2 to 4

Do the same for pages 2, 3 and 4.

The text in the cells must be altered:

Page 2 text:

Home	Page 1	Page 3	Page 4

Page 3 text:

Home	Page 1	Page 2	Page 4

Page 4 text:

Home	Page 1	Page 2	Page 3

Make sure all five pages are saved.

Hyperlinking

The ability to hyperlink pages is one of the great advantages of a website over printed materials.

To make a section of text link to another element in a website you first need to have all the elements saved, as the software can only link to something that has a saved version.

To make links from the home page to the other four pages:

Click and drag on the text 'page 1' in the bottom left cell of the table on the home page.

Click on the Browse for file button next to the Link box of the Properties inspector.

This will open a dialogue box showing your website files. Open the Pages folder and click on the page 1.htm file, then click OK.

The filename and relative address will appear in the Link box.

Below the Link box is a Target box; if you leave this blank and a user clicks on the link the home page will be replaced, in the same window, with page 1. This is normally OK, but you may want it to open in a new window; if you do there is a range of options available from this dropdown.

Make the hyperlinks for the other three pages in exactly the same way.

If the links have been made, the text will be underlined and blue (as the text was blue on this page already, the colour won't appear to change).

Hyperlinks to other pages

Adding the links to the other pages is a little easier.

Open page 1.htm.

Click and drag to highlight the text for the home page and click on the Browse for file button. Navigate to the home page and click OK.

Click and drag to highlight the text 'page 2' and then click on the dropdown arrow in the Link box. The available hyperlinks are stored there, from the links you have made so far.

Because these are relative links, click on pages/page 2.htm and that will appear in the Link box. Delete the text before page 2.htm, as this page is in the same folder as the page you are linking from.

Choose the correct link and then move on to do the page 3 and page 4 links in the same way.

Open page 2.htm and add the links to the correct text. All of the links you will need are now stored in the Link box, so you won't need to navigate to find the correct files.

Do the same for pages 3 and 4.

Make sure all of your pages are saved – File , Save All (ALT+F, SHIFT+L).

Go to your home page and press F12.

Your browser will show the home page and if you click on the text you have just made into hyperlinks, the pages should change.

Check all your links, and if any don't work, go back to your page in Adobe Dreamweaver® and change the link in the Properties inspector.

External hyperlink

The last stage is to add an external hyperlink – this is a link to a page on a website that is not part of the site you have just developed. The link is to the Edexcel site.

On the home page, highlight the text 'Edexcel'.

Click in the Link box and type the link:
http://www.edexcel.org.uk

If it is correct, copy and paste it into the Link box. Click on the dropdown arrow in the Target box and select Blank – this will make the browser open a second window to display the new page.

Save the page and preview it.

The text 'Edexcel' will be underlined and if you click on it a new window will open and if you have access to the Internet, it will display the Edexcel home page.

Experiment

There is a lot more to Adobe Dreamweaver®, some of which you will come across in the *Multimedia* book. But as you now have a simple five-page site, experiment with some of the other tools: add an email link, make the images into 'hotspots' or alter the properties of the tables so that the pages look more interesting.

Tip

To ensure that you have the correct link and the text is exactly right, it may be better to open a browser and check the link by entering it into the address bar.

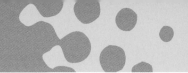

Homework

1 Using the previous structure, produce a full website that gives clear information on the DiDA qualification.

There are a number of DiDA sites available for you to get inspiration, try:

http://dida.edexcel.org.uk/home/

http://www.learn2.co.uk/dida

http://dida.nwlg.org/

2 Develop a structure similar to that above for your e-portfolio; include an index page and then links to each page that you intend to submit.

3 Set up a stopwatch and time the loading of ten websites. Complete the table:

URL	Description	Time to load	Was it worth it?

CHAPTER 19

Word-processing software

What you will learn in this chapter

In this chapter you will learn how to use Microsoft® Word. You will read that Microsoft® Word can do a lot more than write letters and booklets. You will be able to format text, draw and create shapes for diagrams. You will learn how to develop a simple database and create a Mail Merge document. You will read that Microsoft® Word can be used to produce a simple web page.

Introduction

When we talk of word-processing software we really mean software that is specially designed to write with. Programs such as Microsoft®'s WordPad, Word and Notepad are all word processors. These programs replaced typewriters, which relied on accurate typists and did not really allow for mistakes, images or a range of fonts.

Microsoft® Word is probably the best known piece of software in the world, used in millions of homes and businesses. It is used in many countries in the language of that country and is now so powerful you can do just about anything with it!

You can for example make web pages in Microsoft® Word, introduce hyperlinks, draw, paint and create animated text. You can make multiple-choice questionnaires and you can create posters, leaflets, flyers, advertisements, letters and books. This book was written in Microsoft® Word.

It is now so powerful people rarely have any idea of all the things you can do with it. Simply using the keyboard and the mouse and perhaps some clip art you can quickly use Microsoft® Word for constructing letters, posters and booklets.

To summarise, Microsoft® Word can be used for:

- ✦ web pages
- ✦ publications
- ✦ posters
- ✦ flyers
- ✦ postcards
- ✦ as a learning tool if you use it to produce work sheets
- ✦ writing letters
- ✦ a resource for storing web pages
- ✦ drawings
- ✦ diagrams
- ✦ painting
- ✦ sorting lists
- ✦ making graphs
- ✦ creating multiple-choice questionnaires
- ✦ scanning images
- ✦ getting photos from a digital camera
- ✦ simple image editing.

Using Microsoft® Word

Short cuts

Short cuts in Microsoft® Word

The keyboard can be used for more than just typing. It can speed up what is happening on the screen without having to change hands to use the mouse. Using keyboard short cuts allows you to press one, two or three keys to create an action on screen. Short cuts are shown on the drop-down menus. Some you probably all ready know like CONTROL+V = paste.

Counting words in a document

Click into the text block you wish to count, make sure no text is highlighted and select Tools > Word Count. Word displays the number of words and some other statistics for the whole document.

Highlighting a section of text will count words in that selection only. Choose Tools > Word Count. The number of words highlighted will be displayed.

Working with Images

It is possible to do really good image work in Microsoft® Word using the drawing and painting tools, and the image and object manipulation tools. Most of the tools for drawing are found in the Drawing toolbar and the Picture toolbar.

Inserting graphics

Graphics can be images, art or design work, or WordArt that will add value to your text. You can insert several kinds of graphics into a Microsoft® Word document: a graphics file that you have made with Microsoft® Word, clip art that comes with Microsoft® Office, AutoShapes that are also a part of Microsoft® Office programs, or a photo taken with a digital camera. You can also add graphics using a scanner.

To insert a graphics file that you may have created in another application go to Insert > Picture > From File.

Find the file and select it (if it is a picture, click on pictures; if the image is from a camera or scanner, click on the appropriate button on the menu). Click Insert.

Inserting clip art

Choose Insert > Picture > Clip Art. Microsoft® Office has a huge bank of clip art which is often not installed as a default because it takes up a lot of memory, so you may be prompted to insert your Microsoft® Office CD-ROM for more clip art.

Tip

To more easily move a graphics file, insert a text box first. With the text box selected, insert the file. This allows you to move the graphic around the Microsoft® Word page with a mouse instead of a space bar or return key.

Click Insert, when you have found the clip art you need.

The important thing you need to know about clip art is that everyone uses it and some clip-art images are very common and easily spotted. This does not mean you should never use clip art but you need to think carefully about the image you use and whether you could find a better alternative elsewhere. Clip art is brilliant for fast picture finding and is copyright free but is not always the answer.

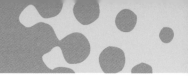

AutoShapes

These are common shapes such as squares, triangles, arrows, flowchart symbols, stars, smiley faces and so on which can be found on the Drawing toolbar. To display the Drawing toolbar you may need to go to View > Toolbars > Drawing.

Choose from the list and then choose the shapes you want to use. Click inside your document where you wish to add the shape. You can also drag to set the size after the shape has been inserted. The 'lines' options allow you to use a range of tools similar to those found in graphics programs such as freehand pencils and polygon tools.

AutoShapes on the Drawing toolbar

Editing graphics

Select the image. This gives you the resizing handles. You can also use the Picture toolbar that appears to modify the image in several ways, including contrast, cropping, brightening, etc.

To change an AutoShape, select it to see the handles. By clicking and dragging the handles, you can resize or stretch it.

Use the shaded area on the edge to drag and move it. (You'll see a four-arrow cursor.)

To remove a graphic, select it and press DELETE.

You can flip or rotate your graphic easily in Microsoft® Word. Free Rotate on the Draw menu of the Drawing toolbar allows you to rotate the shape at any angle. Click and drag the green circles until you have the angle you require.

AutoShapes can be filled with colour by clicking on Fill Colour (a paint bucket) on the Drawing toolbar.

Line Colour can be set using the paintbrush icon on the drawing toolbar. If you fill the shape with a colour, you can remove the line (choose No Line).

Drawing toolbar

Bulleted list

A bulleted list is a common method of listing words or sentences.

Highlight the list you wish to apply bullets to.

To add bullets you go to Format, Bullets and Numbering. Here you can choose from a range of bullet shapes.

Format painter

Formatting has to do with the font, font size, font colour, bold, underlined and so on. If you are likely to use the same formatting over and over you can paint the required formatting over new text instead of adding the same colour and font over and over.

Select the text that has the formatting you want and click on Format Painter on the Standard toolbar.

Select the text you want to format and click and drag the mouse pointer through the text. When you release the mouse button the text will take on the format you chose from elsewhere.

Aligning text

Aligning means lining your text up evenly to the right or left of the text block or to centre the text. To do this highlight the text. Click an alignment button from the Formatting toolbar – Align Left, Centre, Align Right or Justify. Justified text has a straight margin on both sides.

You can align text in advance by clicking on your selected alignment box before you type.

Line spacing

Sometimes the spaces between lines need to be set differently to the standard spacing.

Highlight the paragraphs you wish to change to new line spacing.

To do this you need to click on Format then Paragraph and choose a line-spacing option –

Tip

If you need to format several different sections of text with the same format, choose the text that has the formatting you want and double-click the Format Painter button. Then select all the sections of text that you want to format. Each one will take on the required formatting. Click the Format Painter button again to turn it off.

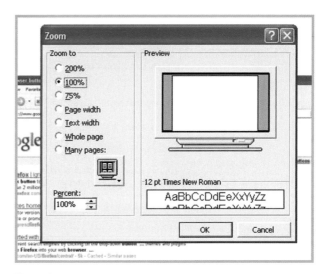

Zooming

single, double and so on. Line spacing is also called 'leading'; this is because years ago strips of the metal lead were used to space out lines in printing presses.

Numbering pages

Numbering pages is an important feature especially if you are producing a publication that has many pages and index. To do this, you must be in Page Layout view. Click the Page Layout button at the bottom left corner of your screen. Select Insert > Page Numbers.

If you have a title page you may not want to display a number on the first page; make sure that the Show Number on First Page box is not ticked.

Styles to format text

Styles can save you a lot of work if you need to have a number of different formats in a long, complex document. Microsoft® Word comes with a large number of styles already created for you but as already mentioned in other sections of this book and the other books in this series, you can easily design your own. Word processing or perhaps desktop publishing are the most likely area of DiDA where you will use styles. If you have prepared a house style which defines fonts, colour, right alignment and so on for different parts of documents, you can set this all up in the style palettes.

Tables

Use tables whenever you want your text to be set up in such a way that it becomes organised or as an alternative to lists.

Tables are very easy to set up and can have either text or graphics placed into them.

Inserting a table

Click on Table from the Standard toolbar. There are two basic methods to create a table: go to Insert then Table and specify the number of columns and rows you need; or select Draw Table and draw a table by dragging out the table as you move your mouse. All tables can be edited.

Adding a row or column

Tip

Always click where you want the new row or column to appear before you select it.

Choose Table > Insert Rows .

To add a row at the very bottom of the table, click in the bottom-right cell and press TAB.

To add columns choose Table > Insert Columns .

You can also right-click over your selected row or column to reveal a menu which gives you the option of Insert Rows or Insert Columns .

Making a database in Microsoft® Word

Go to new document, then insert a table from the Standard toolbar or by choosing Table > Insert Table . Make sure the table has two rows or more and as many columns as you may need for all of your database fields – these could be friends' telephone numbers or addresses. If you have a simple mailing list, you may want these columns: Name, Surname, Town, County/Post code, or four columns.

In row two, type in your data. When you get to the final column, press Tab to make a new row. When you have completed the table of data, save the file with an appropriate name.

This database can be used to carry out an operation called a Mail Merge. Mail Merge is a method of joining data from a database to a word-processed document, such as a letter or a set of address labels. By using this method you can produce one letter – the 'form letter' and combine it with a set of data that can include names and addresses. Microsoft® Word will automatically put the data into the form letter in the position you have allocated.

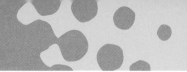

Go to Tools > Letters and Mailings > Mail Merge . You will then see Mail Merge Helper. There is a sequence of six steps to set up a Mail Merge:

1. The first thing to do is to tell the helper what you are doing – in this case producing a standard letter that will be sent to everyone in the address database.

   To set the current page as the main letter, choose Active Window .

2. Link the data with the main document – if you have specified the active window for your document, the Mail Merge Helper then asks you to get the data. Click Get Data .

3. In Open Data Source, find and select your database document that you put together earlier. Click Open .

4. Insert database fields into the main document – Microsoft® Word will tell you that no 'merge fields' have been found in your main document. These are the placeholders for the data from your database.

   So click Edit Main Document .

5. Microsoft® Word will return you to the main document. A new toolbar (the Mail Merge toolbar) will appear at the top of the document.

   Move your cursor to where you want to have data inserted in your main document and click on the Insert Merge Field button. If you need a space between lines, press ENTER, or use punctuation. For example, if you have 'First Name' plus 'Last Name' fields, after you have inserted the 'First Name' field, you might want to press the spacebar before inserting the 'Last Name' field.

   You should also format the text at this point; if you choose to make the merge field bold, the formatting will be carried over onto the data when it is inserted.

6. Preview the inserted data by clicking on the View Merged Data button on the Mail Merge toolbar. If you are happy that the data is correct and is formatted as you want it you can then continue and run the Mail Merge. If you are not happy, click on the View Merged Data button again to go back to the merge fields and edit as necessary.

When you are running the merge you have a number of options:

✦ Merge straight to the printer; this is fine if you want to print out the letters.

✦ Merge to a new document; this will produce an electronic copy.

✦ Merge to email or merge to fax will send copies to the respective applications.

> **Tip**
>
> Don't merge to printer unless you are absolutely sure that the merge is perfect!

Viewing documents

A document is what you are working on. We sometimes also call it a file. As we have already mentioned, you should always zoom in if you can to reduce eye strain. Sometimes in order to see what your layout looks like you may zoom out to see the whole page.

Your document can be displayed on screen in four ways. The small buttons at the bottom-left corner of your screen allow you to see your file differently in preset formats:

✦ Normal View – shows just plain text, no margins, headers, footers or page numbers.

✦ Web Layout View – text is displayed larger than in Page Layout view and wraps to fit the window; there is also a document map that gives shortcuts to different parts of the document.

✦ Page Layout View – shows the whole document as it will be if printed.

✦ Outline View – helps you to view the structure of a document.

Finding a document

This can waste a lot of your time especially if you are looking to work on DiDA documents you saved last year or a while ago.

If you cannot remember the name or location of a document, you can have Microsoft® Word search for the document by text contained in the document filename.

Go to File menu then click Tools > Open .

Use the Look in: drop-down list to choose the drive or folder you want to search.

At the bottom of the dialogue box you will need to enter a string of text that could be found in the document filename. For example, if you know that the document filename contains the word 'Fred', type Fred.

Click Find Now and Microsoft® Word will list all filenames that contain the word Fred.

Save and preview as a web page

Create a web page

Microsoft® Word can be used for designing and setting up a web page in very much the way you would design a page for a magazine. You can add the hyperlinks which are detailed elsewhere in this book and then Save as Web Page instead of as a normal document. This can then be previewed in a browser; click Web Page Preview. It also gives you an image of options such as scrolling text for web pages.

Remember anything you do in Microsoft® Word can be placed into other applications such as Microsoft PowerPoint®, Microsoft Excel® and most other applications you are likely to come across.

Homework

1 Design a simple text page for a DiDA project front cover, save it as a web page then view it through a browser. Try adding a scanned image.

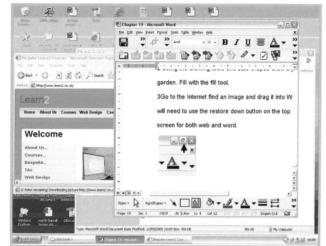

Drag an image from the Internet into Microsoft® Word

2 Using the drawing tools and AutoShapes redraw a plan of your garden as a garden designer might. Try to add some crazy features. Fill with the Fill Colour tool.

3 Go to the Internet, find an image and drag it into Microsoft® Word using the mouse.

You will need to use the Restore Down button on the top right-hand side of your screen for both web and Microsoft® Word.

Restore Down button

Summative project brief

The final marks you are awarded are based on the summative project brief (SPB). The SPB is the project that the exam board sends to you in the final year of your course. The brief will be posted on the Edexcel website, and your teacher will explain what you need to do. The brief asks you to solve a problem by using the skills and knowledge you have acquired during your DiDA course to produce a piece of work.

It is recommended that a minimum of 30 hours should be spent working on this brief – your teacher may allow you a little more time. It must be clear to the board that you have done the work yourself and that the work was supervised by a member of staff qualified to do so. The final product must be your own work.

Your SPB could be built up in the following sequence, perhaps as a series of mini projects:

✦ gathering information

✦ planning

✦ researching

✦ creating a database

✦ market research

✦ graphics

✦ a presentation and final report.

It is very important that you always save your work carefully and keep a backup. If you lose your work it cannot be marked. If it is saved but difficult to retrieve, you will lose marks. If you fail to complete a part, you will lose marks.

There are details on the e-portfolio elsewhere in this book (specifically, Chapter 8), and there is information available from the awarding body – make sure you check the details with your teacher.

Create a folder for your project, then you can create further folders within it for specific types of work, such as graphics, databases, research and so on.

Practice project

You are to produce a business proposal that sets out clearly a plan to create a breakfast club in five local secondary schools. You should produce a feasibility study and demonstrate that there is a demand from parents to drop children off at their schools earlier.

The proposal should include:

✦ a detailed business plan

✦ a feasibility study

✦ a health and safety code

✦ a presentation that would convince the head teachers and governors of the schools

✦ evidence that the business will provide a safe, healthy and interesting environment for the children

✦ one brochure for parents and one for children.

You should create a website to show that the business is sound and would benefit the schools. You will also need to look into the legal issues relating to working with children.

All items must total less than 15 MB.

When producing these products you should remind yourself of the audience and the purpose. Not everyone taking part in the project has English as a first language, so it would be inappropriate to rely too much on text or speech.

To ensure that your audience enjoys looking at your materials, you need to ensure that they work well – that means using prototypes throughout the development of your products, and testing them with users. If your products are effective, you will have demonstrated your ability to apply your ICT skills in the best possible way.

Before anything else, you should prepare a work plan, which addresses the following questions:

✦ What information do I need to gather?

✦ How can it be presented?

✦ Who will it be presented to?

✦ What software is available?

✦ How can I store the information?

✦ What do I need to do first?

Your plan could be produced as a single-sided document, with hyperlinks to various files or folders.

What information do I need?

You will need to collect information about the needs of this age range, such as reading level, what vocabulary would be suitable, range of languages and what visual information would be appropriate.

You may need to find experts who are coordinating the planning and development of similar clubs across the country.

You will need to gather a variety of multimedia components for use in your product. You must produce some of the components yourself and use some that are ready-made. These components could include video clips, audio clips, text and images. You may be able to use a component in more than one product.

How can it be presented and who will it be presented to?

You need to enter the information into an application that will allow you to manipulate it to produce the graphics and data required. You will have access to a range of facilities to test your products, but most of your project will need to be displayed on a screen, on printed matter or through a standard browser.

You will need to decide how best to present the information to make sure that the audience is able to understand it, and interested enough to want to learn more.

What software is available?

You should check with your teacher if you are unsure, but you should have access to Microsoft Office® applications (or similar), as well as image manipulation, sound recording, video editing, web design, animation and other software.

How can I store the information?

Your teacher will allocate an area on the school system for you to save your work, but you will have to set up a file or folder structure yourself. Remember to keep regular backups.

What do I need to do first?

Start by planning what you are going to do and developing a realistic timeline. Build in time to collect components and generate your own resources, as well as manipulating them and combining them for the products.

Hints and tips

✦ Remember, a picture paints a thousand words – use images and video where you can to illustrate a particular idea. Do not rely on the audience reading text.

✦ If something does not add anything to your product, it probably detracts from it – nothing distracts like a big transition fanfare to celebrate the pressing of the `Next` button.

✦ Do not use fonts that are complex – stick to simple, easy-to-read typefaces. Some experts recommend a font designed specifically for online viewing, such as Arial, while others would choose readable classic fonts, such as Goudy. Remember that ornate or very 'blocky' fonts are difficult to read on-screen. Keep the font size as large as possible.

✦ WordArt has its place, but less is generally more in a financial presentation. It has been suggested that overuse of WordArt is the mark of an amateur.

✦ Choose colours with care: a black or dark-blue background and white or light-yellow text is easy to read. However, most people prefer black text on a white background – although the white background is somewhat harsher, it is easier to see in a room with more light.

✦ Background designs need to be simple. Make sure they do not overlap and obscure your information. Think about the quality of the screen your audience will be using. Beautiful backgrounds and colours may not look the same on a low-resolution screen as they do on your computer – another reason to keep your backgrounds simple.

✦ Check for unintended colour combinations and symbols – unless you are presenting financial statements for a doll-making company, you should avoid pink!

✦ Do not beat about the bush! Assume that your audience is busy and intelligent.

Evaluation

When you have finished your multimedia products, review your work. Is it fit for purpose? How well does it meet the needs of the audience? How could it be improved?

You should also evaluate your work throughout the project. How well did your plan work? What did you learn from the prototype? What went wrong, and why? Is there anything you would do differently?

If you have been keeping a quality log, you should have a record of the feedback you received while working on the project. You need to use that feedback to inform your choices.

Your evaluation could be a written report, but you could also make use of:

✦ video clips

✦ audio clips

✦ presentations.

How do I get good marks?

✓ **Look at the brief regularly and stick to it.**

✓ **Research thoroughly and keep it relevant.**

✓ **Remember your aims and keep them in mind at all times.**

✓ **Test and evaluate regularly.**

✓ **Ask your friends and family to look at what you have done and ask for feedback. Use constructive criticism to improve your project.**

✓ **Check your planning notes and timeline regularly.**

✓ **Make sure you include elements from each software group.**

✓ **Ensure your work is easy for others to access and understand.**

Analogue – signals which vary continuously for example temperature readings from a sensor.

Application – A piece of software which fulfils a particular, and often specific, task; examples are spreadsheets, word processors, graphics software.

ASCII – American Standard Code for Information Interchange – this is a coding system used to represent characters by using numbers.

Backup File – This is a copy of an original used in case the original is corrupted, damaged or lost.

Bit – The smallest unit of data which represents one character. Bits are only ever either '1' or '0'.

Bitmap – An image which is created in a specialised graphics package, such as Microsoft Paint®. This type of file takes up a lot of memory.

Broadband – This is the term given to fast Internet connections which allow the transportation of large amounts of data quickly.

Browser – A piece of software that is used to access web pages.

CD-ROM – A type of storage medium used to hold large amounts of data. It is used for transportation and archiving large files such as images, presentations and large publications. These files cannot be edited as the user

will only have write-read access.

Clickable image – any image which when clicked with a mouse causes some form of action to take place.

Compression – Reducing the size of a large file (often used to reduce the size of large image files).

Co-processor – A microchip that handles a specific task. The fact that it is dedicated to a task means the computer can work on other processes.

Crash – A problem arising when the computer stops working as it should.

Cursor – the pointer that is used to represent the mouse on the screen.

Dialogue box – a window that displays options from which the user can make choices.

Dial-up line – a standard phone line used to connect a computer to the Internet. As the name suggests, a connection has to be made each time you wish to use this.

Digital – a series of pulses in discrete levels.

Directory – a structured area that visually represents the files stored in the computer's memory.

Download – to obtain a file from another computer

DPI – dots per inch – a unit of measurement used to describe the resolution of an image.

DTP – Desk Top Publishing

Email – electronic mail, used to send messages from one computer user to another.

File – information stored on a disk in a particular, predefined format.

Firewall – a means of preventing unwanted intrusion onto a network which is connected to the Internet.

Flatbed scanner – A scanning device that lies flat on a desk – useful for creating digital versions of text documents or images from printed originals.

Folder – An area in which files or other folders are stored.

Font – a style of text.

FTP – File Transfer Protocol – the means by which files are transferred across a network.

GIF – Graphic Interchange Format – a file format used for images.

Graphical user interface (GUI) – The visual representation of the computer system which it easier for users to run applications and carry out computer-related tasks.

Homepage – the main page of any web site.

Host – the main computer to which users are connected.

Hostname – the name which identifies each computer attached to the Internet.

HTML – Hyper Text Markup Language – this used to show

browsers how to portray web pages on the screen.

Hypertext – a means of linking phrases or images on one webpage to other pages or files simply by clicking on them.

Import – to bring data from one document and place it into another document.

Internet – The world's largest network.

Java – A programming language used to create applications that can run within web pages.

JPEG – Joint Photographic Experts Group – a format used for graphics files, particularly photographs.

kB – kilobyte is a unit of data storage

LAN – Local Area Network – a network that is situated within a single site or location.

Line art – images which are not photographs shown in only black and white.

Mail merge – Merging data from a database into a document template to create an individual, automated, personalised document.

Mailing list – list of members of a particular email group.

Memory – the chips where data is stored on a computer.

Menu – list of commands.

Menu bar – the bar on which the menus are displayed.

Modem – A device used to connect a computer to the telephone sytem in order to utilise the internet.

MOV – a file extension used to denote a file created in Quicktime.

MPEG – Moving Pictures Expert Group – international standard for video compression. Requires a specialised movie player to be installed on the computer.

Multimedia – a presentation or software that combines a range of media types.

Navigation tools – allows users to find their way around a web site.

Network – a group of computers that are connected in one of a series of ways to form LANs or WANs.

Object–oriented – describes illustrations that are created by mathematical equations.

OCR – Optical Character Recognition – used to scan text from a printed document and convert into digital form so that it can be imported into an application such as a word processor.

On-line – any computer that is connected to another computer.

Operating system – the software which controls the tasks on a computer.

Paste – to insert images or text from another source.

Path – a route used to find files stored on a disk.

PDF – Portable Document Format – used to create documents that can be read on any platform of computer – access to a small plug-in is a all that is required to read the document.

Pixel – Picture element – images are made up of pixels.

Plug-in – small programs that are required to run some web-based applications.

Properties – information about an object or file.

Protocols – the rules governing how data is transmitted between devices.

Quicktime – a file extension for movies.

RAM – Random Access Memory. This is the most common type of computer memory and is used to store programs which are being used at the time.

Resolution – this refers to the sharpness of the images that are being shown.

ROM – Read Only Memory – permanent information is stored here.

Scanner – a device used to convert paper-based originals into digital format.

Search engines – web utilities that are used to help a user to find the answer to a query from huge databases of information.

Site – the location of a host.

Spreadsheet – a number-related table which can have calculations applied to it.

SQL – Structured Query Language – the language used by many database systems.

Tags – the formatting codes used in HTML to define the way that content is displayed by a browser.

Taskbar – the bottom of the screen where currently loaded documents and software are displayed.

TIFF – Tag Image File Format – these files are also bitmaps and are their versatility makes them, suitable for transferring files between different applications.

Title bar – the top of a window which contains a name.

Upload – to send a file to another computer.

URL – Uniform Resource Locator – a string of characters that makes up the unique address of a web page.

Web browser – allows you to access HTML documents.

Webpage – the visual representation of HTML codes, text and images.

Word processing – manipulation of text to create documents.

Zipped – compressed version of a program or document.

Index

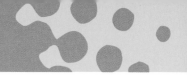

ICT in Enterprise Student's CD-ROM

The enclosed single-user licence CD-ROM contains various resources designed to assist your throughout your course. The CD-ROM has several features, including sections that correspond to the chapters in this textbook. These features include:

◆ Exercises: there are one or two exercises in this section for each chapter of the textbook. Each one will help you to consolidate your knowledge of a particular topic. Some require you to refer to a specific website, for others there are associated files that you can use to complete the exercise. Whenever associated files are mentioned in an exercise they are written in CAPITALS and a link to the file itself will appear in the 'Resource File' panel on the right-hand side of the page.

◆ Tutorials: These demonstrations of how to use various software packages are available in those chapters (13-16) that relate directly to software applications. Short descriptions of each skill will appear when you roll the mouse pointer over each tutorial link.

◆ Useful links: this section contains useful links to other websites and resources relevant to each particular topic. If you are connected to the Internet, simply clicking on each link will open the website in a new web browser window. *Please note: All weblinks contain live content and information, and as such this content is liable to change. Hodder & Stoughton Ltd are not responsible for the content of any external website. An assessment of the appropriateness of each website for the intended audience should be undertaken by a responsible adult.*

◆ Resource bank: This area provides a range of dummy files for you to practise your software skills on. They are nothing more than examples of each type of file, to help you to get used to the sorts of files you will be working with when studying DiDA Unit 4. You can take each file and do whatever you want with it – stretch it, squash it, edit it, delete it...! Some of these files are duplicates of those that are used in exercises from the student and teacher sections; other files only appear in this section.

Before you start using this CD-ROM, it may be helpful to refer to the 'How to use this CD-ROM' section, which you can access from the main menu screen. Included in this area is a tutorial that will provide you with a step-by-step introduction to accessing and using the different types of resources available on this CD-ROM.

ELECTRONIC END USER SINGLE USE LICENCE AGREEMENT

FOR **DiDA Unit 4: ICT in Enterprise CD-ROM Student Version** software published by Hodder and Stoughton Limited (HS) under its Hodder Arnold imprint.

NOTICE TO USER:
THIS IS A CONTRACT. BY INSTALLING THIS SOFTWARE YOU AND OTHERS TO WHOM YOU ALLOW ACCESS TO THE SOFTWARE ACCEPT ALL THE TERMS AND CONDITIONS OF THIS AGREEMENT.

This End User Single Use Licence Agreement accompanies the **DiDA Unit 4: ICT in Enterprise CD-ROM Student Version** software (the Software) and shall also apply to any upgrades, modified versions or updates of the Software licensed to you by HS. Please read this Agreement carefully. Upon installing this software you will be asked to accept this Agreement and continue to install or, if you do not wish to accept this Agreement, to decline this Agreement, in which case you will not be able to use the Software.

Upon your acceptance of this Agreement, HS grants to you a non-exclusive, non-transferable licence to install, run and use the Software, subject to the following:

1. Use of the Software. **You may only install a single copy of the Software onto the hard disk or other storage device of only one computer**. If the computer is linked to a local area network then it must be installed in such a way so that the Software cannot be accessed by other computers on the same network. You may make a single back-up copy of the Software (which must be deleted or destroyed on expiry or termination of this Agreement). Except for that single back-up copy, you may not make or distribute any copies of the Software, or use it in any way not specified in this Agreement.

2. Copyright. The Software is owned by HS and its authors and suppliers, and is protected by Copyright Law. Except as stated above, this Agreement does not grant you any intellectual property rights in the Software or in the contents of **DiDA Unit 4: ICT in Enterprise CD-ROM Student Version** as sold. All moral rights of artists and all other contributors to the Software are hereby asserted.

3. Restrictions. You assume full responsibility for the use of the Software and agree to use the Software legally and responsibly. You agree that you or any other person within or acting on behalf of the purchasing institution shall NOT: use or copy the Software otherwise than as specified in clause 1; transfer, distribute, rent, loan, lease, sub-lease or otherwise deal in the Software or any part of it; alter, adapt, merge, modify or translate the whole or any part of the Software for any purpose; or permit the whole or any part of the Software to be combined with or incorporated in any other product or program. You agree not to reverse engineer, decompile, disassemble or otherwise attempt to discover the source code of the Software. You may not alter or modify the installer program or any other part of the Software or create a new installer for the Software.

4. No Warranty. The Software is being delivered to you AS IS and HS makes no warranty as to its use or performance except that the Software will perform substantially as specified. HS AND ITS AUTHORS AND SUPPLIERS DO NOT AND CANNOT GIVE ANY WARRANTY REGARDING THE PERFORMANCE OR RESULTS YOU MAY OBTAIN BY USING THE SOFTWARE OR ACCOMPANYING OR DERIVED DOCUMENTATION. HS AND ITS AUTHORS AND SUPPLIERS MAKE NO WARRANTIES, EXPRESS OR IMPLIED, AS TO NON-INFRINGEMENT OF THIRD PARTY RIGHTS, THE CONTENT OF THE SOFTWARE, MERCHANTABILITY, OR FITNESS FOR ANY PARTICULAR PURPOSE. IN NO EVENT WILL HS OR ITS AUTHORS OR SUPPLIERS BE LIABLE TO YOU FOR ANY CONSEQUENTIAL, INCIDENTAL, SPECIAL OR OTHER DAMAGES, OR FOR ANY CLAIM BY ANY THIRD PARTY (INCLUDING PERSONS WITH WHOM YOU HAVE USED THE SOFTWARE TO PROVIDE LEARNING SUPPORT) ARISING OUT OF YOUR INSTALLATION OR USE OF THE SOFTWARE.

5. Entire liability. HS's entire liability, and your sole remedy for a breach of the warranty given under Clause 4, is (a) the replacement of the Software not meeting the above limited warranty and which is returned by you within 90 days of purchase; or (b) if HS or its distributors are unable to deliver a replacement copy of the Software you may terminate this Agreement by returning the Software within 90 days of purchase and your money will be refunded. All other liabilities of HS including, without limitation, indirect, consequential and economic loss and loss of profits, together with all warranties, are hereby excluded to the fullest extent permitted by law.

6. Governing Law and General Provisions. This Agreement shall be governed by the laws of England and any actions arising shall be brought before the courts of England. If any part of this Agreement is found void and unenforceable, it will not affect the validity of the balance of the Agreement, which shall remain wholly valid and enforceable according to its terms. All rights not specifically licensed to you under this Agreement are reserved to HS. This Agreement shall automatically terminate upon failure by you to comply with its terms. This Agreement is the entire and only agreement between the parties relating to its subject matter. It supersedes any and all previous agreements and understandings (whether written or oral) relating to its subject matter and may only be amended in writing, signed on behalf of both parties.